ORIGAMI
FOR KIDS

Learning
THROUGH ACTIVITIES

SPECIAL BONUS!

Want The Video Tutorials For FREE?

Get **FREE** access to every video tutorial of each Origami Design by joining our community!

Scan W/ Your Camera To Get The Videos!

Table of Contents

Introduction.................. 1

Symbols..................... 2

Dog.......................... 3

Fox.......................... 4

Cat.......................... 5

Mouse...................... 6

Boat......................... 7

Rabbit...................... 9

Pig..........................10

Plane....................... 11

Crab........................ 13

Heart....................... 15

Penguin.................... 16

Ladybug................... 17

Turtle...................... 19

Fish I....................... 21

Fish II...................... 22

Star........................ 23

Car......................... 25

Rocket..................... 27

Shirt....................... 29

Snake...................... 31

Ice Cream................. 33

Butterfly................... 35

Bat......................... 37

Bookmark................. 39

Whale...................... 40

Dolphin.................... 41

Table of Contents

Bird...................... 43

Seal 45

Crane 47

Seahorse 49

Hummingbird........... 51

Lotus Flower............ 53

Brachiosaurus 55

Elephant 59

Dragon 63

Pop-it Toy 67

Fish III 69

Peacock 71

Frog 77

Tulip 79

Koala.................... 81

Carrot 83

Box 85

Ninja Star I.............. 87

Triceratops.............. 89

Ninja Star II............. 95

Magic Circle........... 97

Water Lily 99

Christmas Tree.......... 101

Pop-it Triangle........105

Conclusion 109

Introduction

Origami is the art of transforming a sheet of paper, usually square but also rectangular, into a sculpture without using other instruments, such as scissors or glue.

This technique helps improve concentration, abstract thinking, fine motor skills, and hand-eye coordination, besides promoting creativity. Emotionally speaking, it is a great activity to relax and improve patience.

In 'Origami for Kids' you will find 50 impressive designs to immerse yourself in this new and wonderful hobby that is paper folding. Starting with simple designs, you will take giant steps until you become an expert and tackle more and more complex ones. You will even learn to make figures that involve more than one paper sheet!

Are you ready to discover this new world? Let the fun begin!

Symbols

Lines

--------------- Valley fold, fold forward.

.... Mountain fold, fold backward.

_____ Crease line.

Arrows

 Fold in this direction.

 Turn over.

  Shows the result after each step.

Paper

Square sheet	Rectangular sheet	All sheets have two shades to better show each step.

Dog

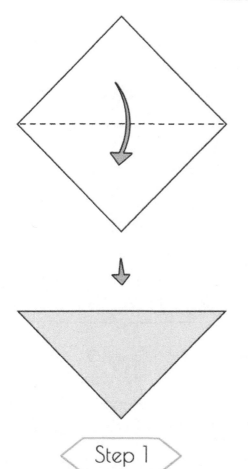

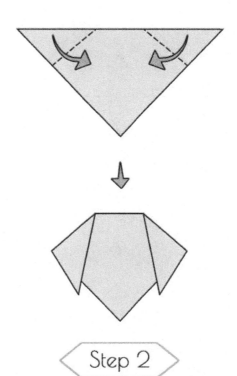

Fold the sheet down along
one of its diagonals.

Step 2

Fold the side corners at
an angle so that they
stick out at the bottom.

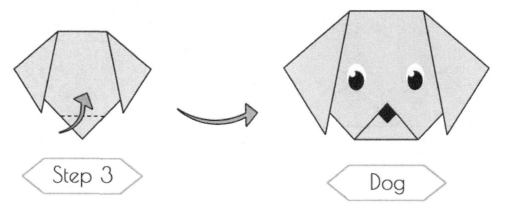

Step 3

Fold the bottom corner
up both sides of the paper
at the same time.

Dog

3

Fox

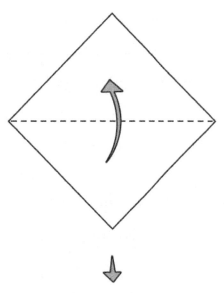

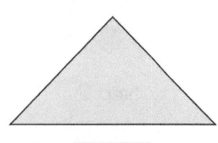

Fold the sheet up along
one of its diagonals.

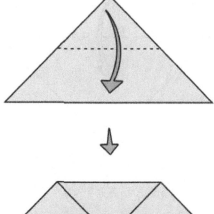

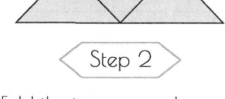

Step 2

Fold the top corner down all
the way to the bottom edge.

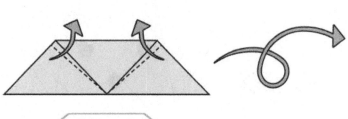

Step 3

Fold the side corners so that their
vertices end up pointing up.

Fox

4

Cat

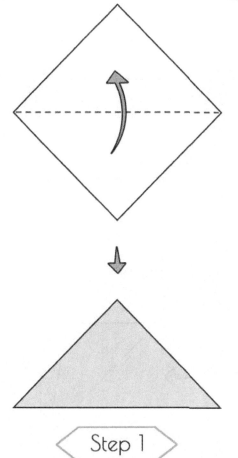

Step 1

Fold the sheet up along
one of its diagonals.

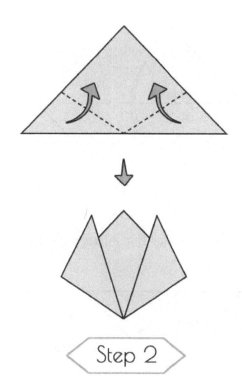

Step 2

Fold the side corners so that their
vertices end up pointing up, and there
is some space left between them.

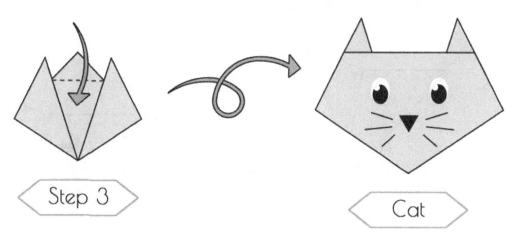

Step 3

Fold the top corner all the way down to
the flaps you made in the previous step.

Cat

Mouse

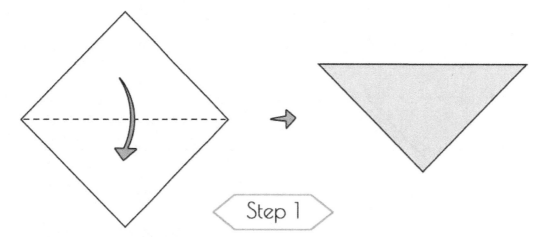

Step 1

Fold the sheet down along one of its diagonals.

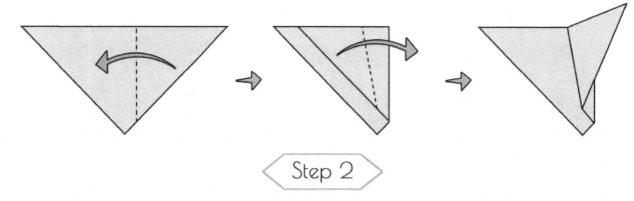

Step 2

Fold a little less than the right half of the triangle inward. Then fold a part of that flap out again, but this time at a slight angle.

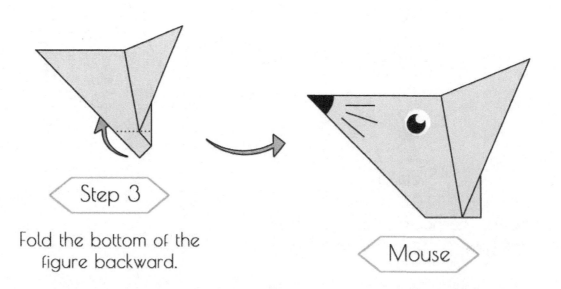

Step 3

Fold the bottom of the figure backward.

Mouse

Boat

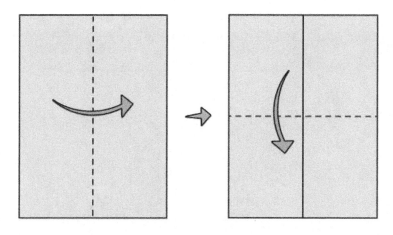

Step 1

Fold in half lengthwise and unfold. Then fold in half crosswise.

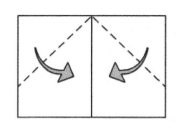 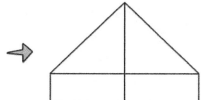

Step 2

Fold both corners forward.

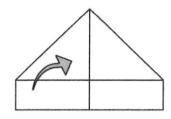 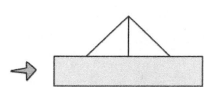

Step 3

Fold up the bottom edges of both sides of the sheet.

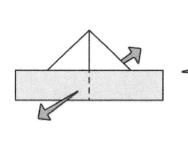 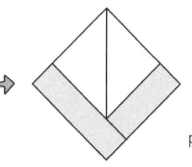

Step 4

From the midline, pull out in opposite directions and press to get a diamond shape.

Boat

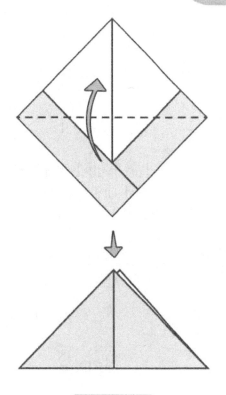

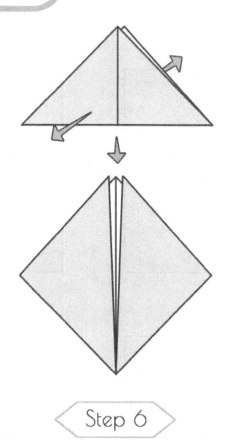

Fold up the bottom halves of both **faces** to get a triangle.

Again, pull out from the midline and flatten to get a diamond shape with two flaps.

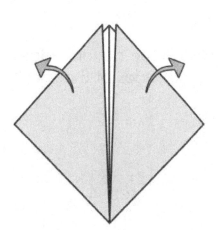

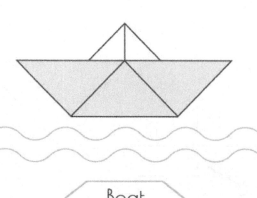

Pull the flaps to the sides and press.

Boat

Rabbit

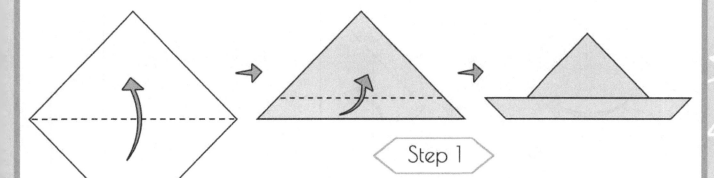

Step 1

Fold the sheet up along one of its diagonals,
then fold the bottom edge up.

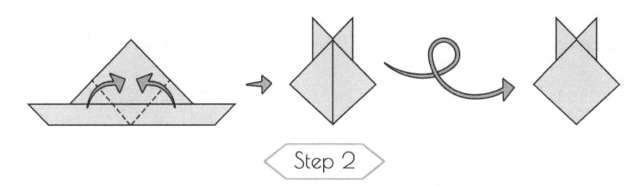

Step 2

Bring both side corners in toward the midline, and turn the figure over.

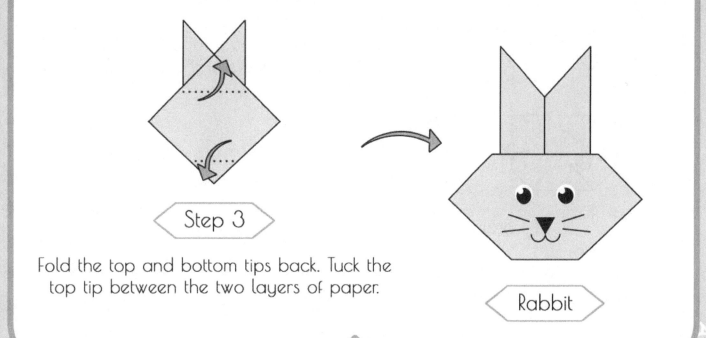

Step 3

Fold the top and bottom tips back. Tuck the
top tip between the two layers of paper.

Rabbit

Pig

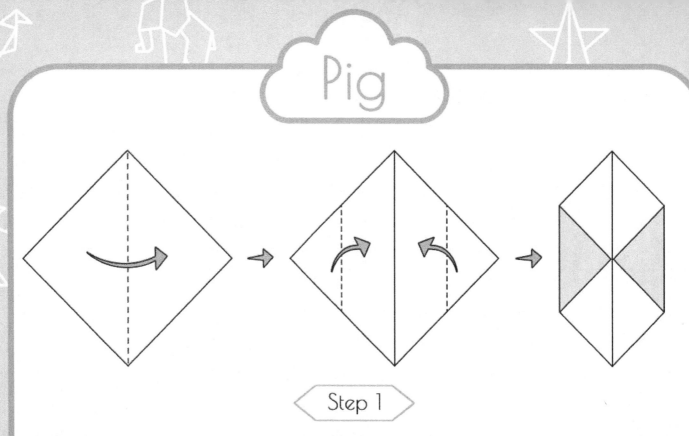

Step 1

Fold along a diagonal and unfold. Then bring the side corners to the midline.

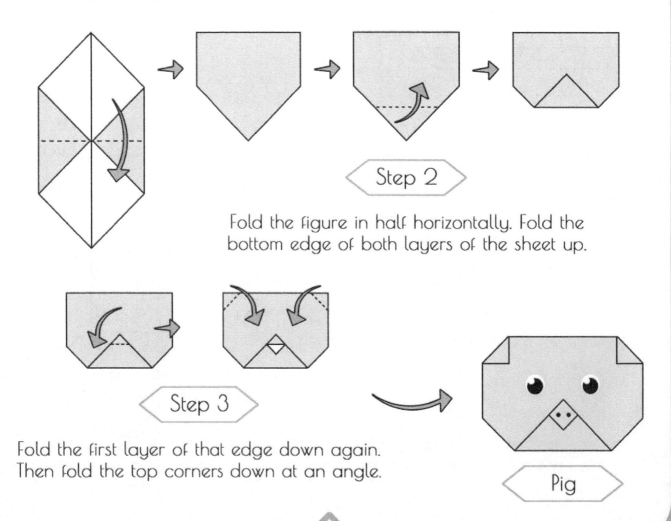

Step 2

Fold the figure in half horizontally. Fold the bottom edge of both layers of the sheet up.

Step 3

Fold the first layer of that edge down again. Then fold the top corners down at an angle.

Pig

Plane

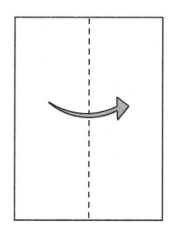

Fold the paper sheet
in half lengthwise
and then unfold it.

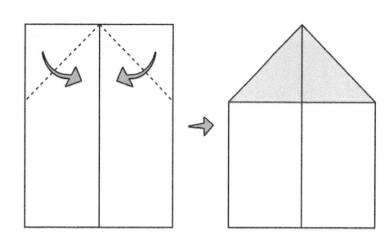

Bring the top corners down
to the center line.

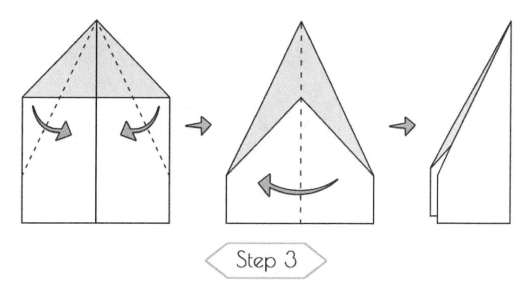

Step 3

Bring the top corners down to the center line. Then fold the
plane in half along the crease you made in the first step.

11

Plane

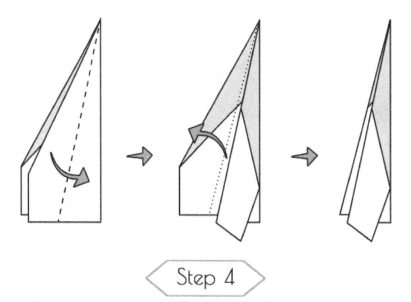

Fold one wing down along its center line,
repeat with the other wing, and press.

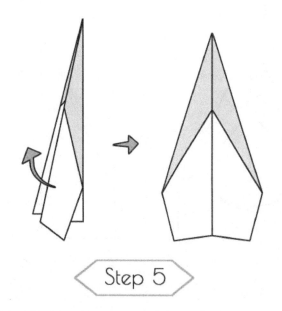

Step 5

Unfold both wings halfway up so
they are perpendicular to the plane.

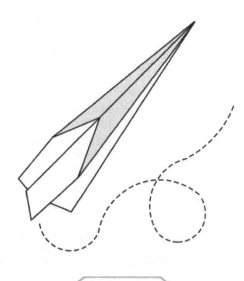

Plane

12

Crab

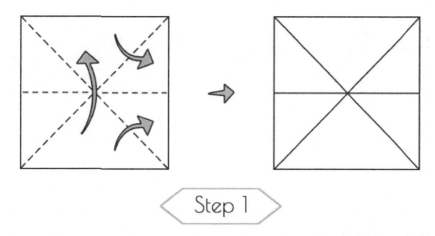

Step 1

Fold in half crosswise and along the two diagonals, then unfold.

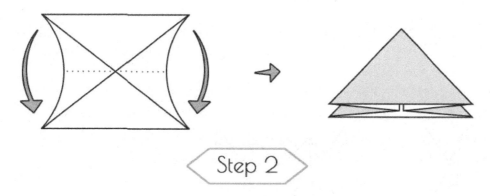

Step 2

Fold the sides to the center and flatten to get a triangle.

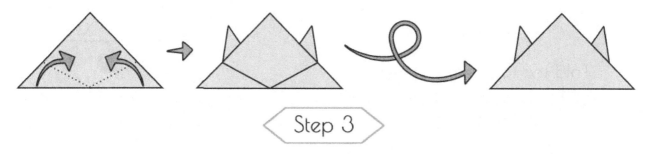

Step 3

Fold the side corners of the top layer inward
at a slight angle and turn the figure over.

13

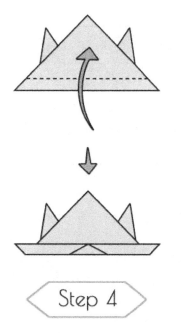

Step 4

Fold the bottom edge up.

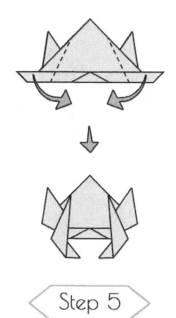

Step 5

Fold the side corners of the top layer inward at a slight angle.

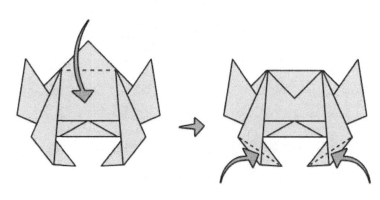

Step 6

Fold the top corner down, then fold the bottom legs in half and flip the figure over.

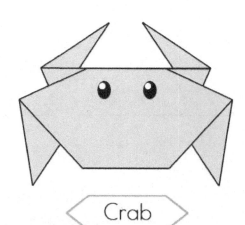

Crab

Heart

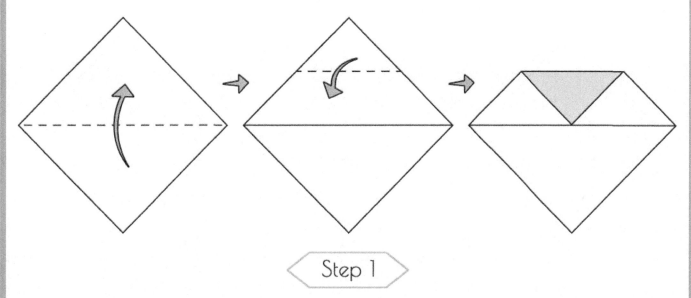

Step 1

Fold along a diagonal and unfold. Then fold the top corner toward the midline.

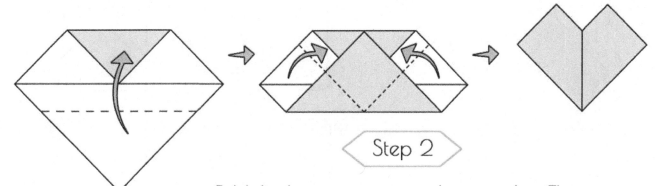

Step 2

Fold the bottom corner to the top edge. Then fold both sides at an angle toward the midline.

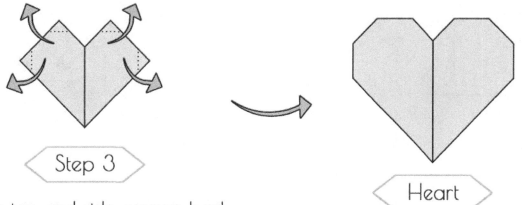

Step 3

Fold the top and side corners back.

Heart

Penguin

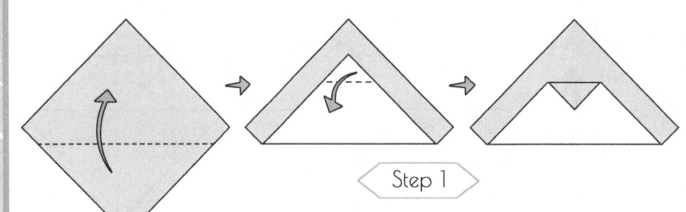

Step 1

Fold the bottom part up to just below the midline, then fold the tip of that same corner down.

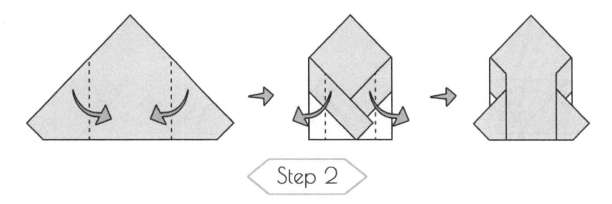

Step 2

Flip the sheet over and fold the side corners in so they overlap, then fold half of those flaps out again.

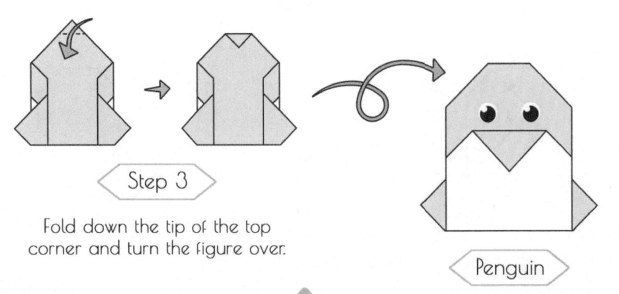

Step 3

Fold down the tip of the top corner and turn the figure over.

Penguin

Ladybug

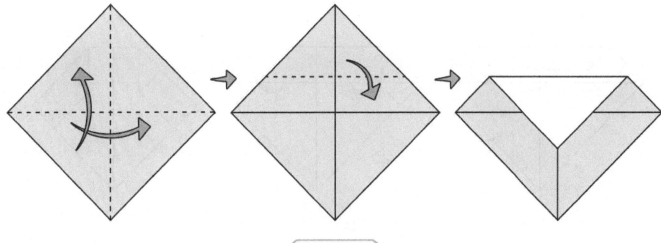

Fold along both diagonals and unfold. Then fold the top corner down to just below the midline.

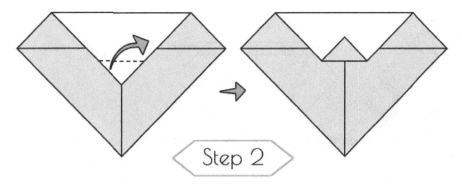

Step 2

Fold the tip of that same corner up and forward.

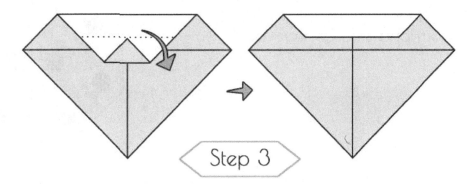

Step 3

Fold that section again, up and backward this time.

Ladybug

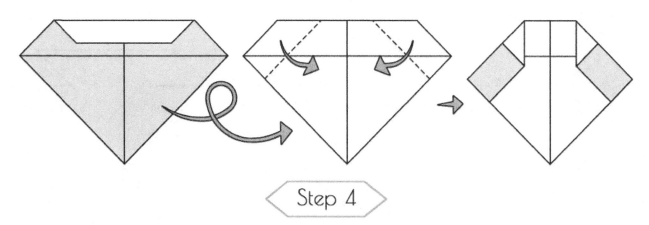

Step 4

Turn the figure over and fold the side corners at an angle
so that the top edge ends up parallel to the midline.

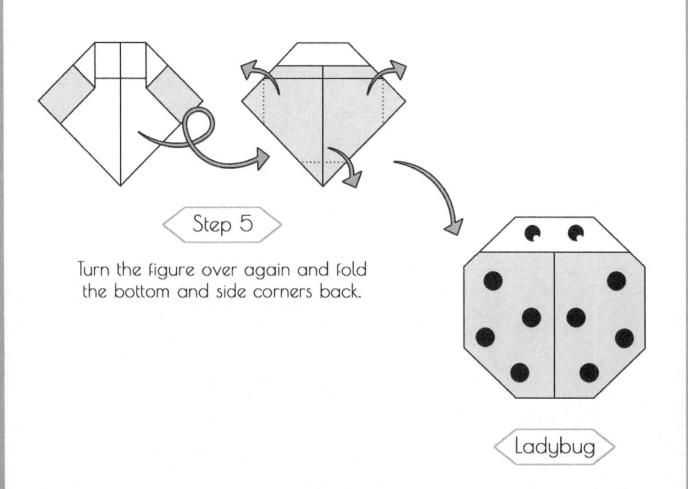

Step 5

Turn the figure over again and fold
the bottom and side corners back.

Ladybug

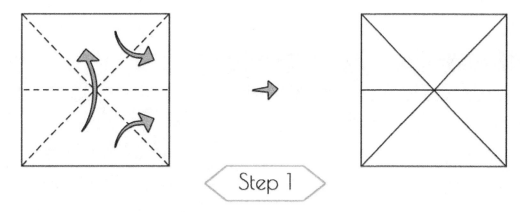

Step 1

Fold in half crosswise and along the two diagonals, then unfold.

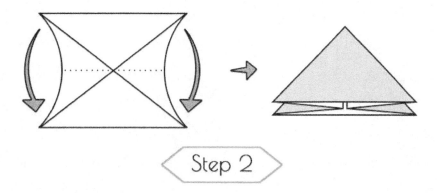

Step 2

Fold both sides in towards the center and press the edges to make a triangle.

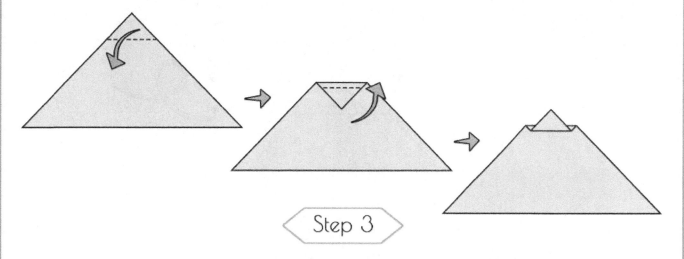

Step 3

Fold the top corner down, then fold it up again to make the head.

Turtle

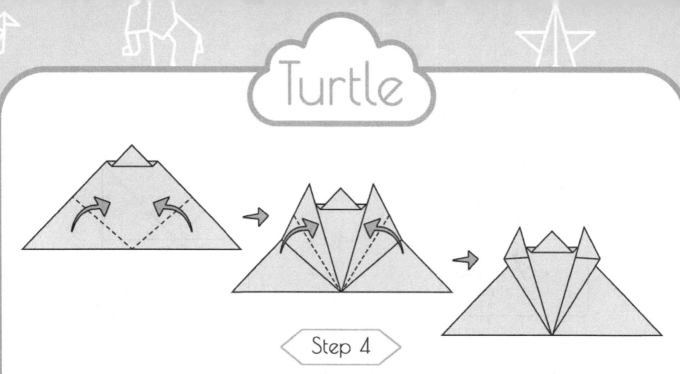

Fold the sides of the top layer of the triangle towards the head. Fold these flaps you just made in half again towards the head. These are the front legs.

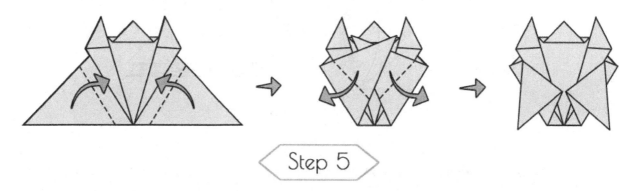

Step 5

Fold the sides of the triangle up, parallel to the front legs you just made. Then fold the tip down at an angle so that the tips stick out the sides.

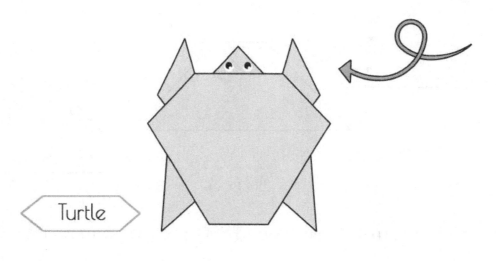

Turtle

Fish

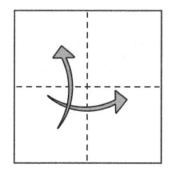

Step 1

Fold in half lengthwise
and crosswise, and unfold.

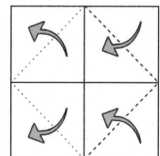

Step 2

Fold the two left corners backward
and the two right corners forward,
and press the edges.

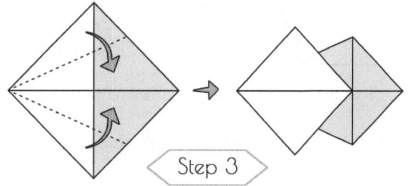

Step 3

Bring the top and bottom corners to the midline and press the edges.
You will see the corners that we folded backward sticking out from the sides.

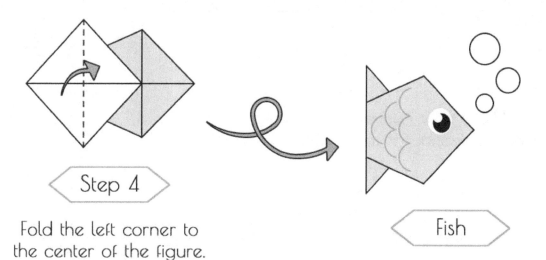

Step 4

Fold the left corner to
the center of the figure.

Fish

Fish

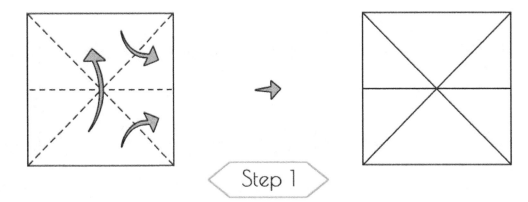

Step 1

Fold in half crosswise and along the two diagonals, then unfold.

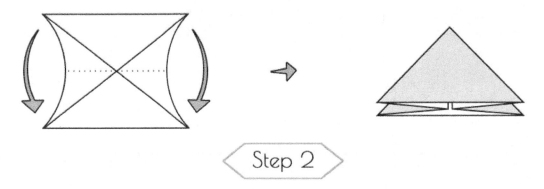

Step 2

Fold the sides to the center and flatten to get a triangle.

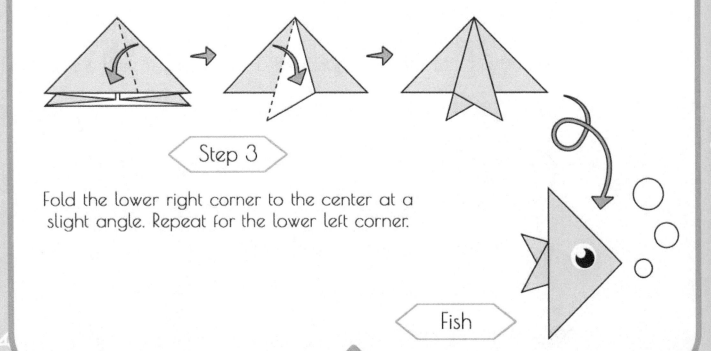

Step 3

Fold the lower right corner to the center at a slight angle. Repeat for the lower left corner.

Fish

Star

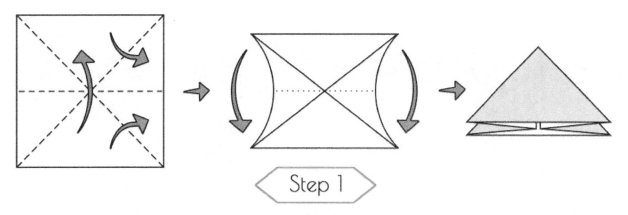

Step 1

Fold in half crosswise and along the two diagonals, and unfold. Then fold both sides in toward the center and press the edges to make a triangle.

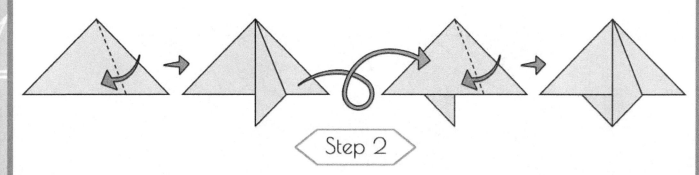

Step 2

Fold the right corner of the top layer toward the midline and press. Turn the figure over and repeat the same step with the back right corner.

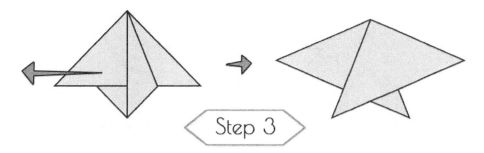

Step 3

Pull the left corner to expand the figure until the two flaps you made in the previous step swap their positions.

Star

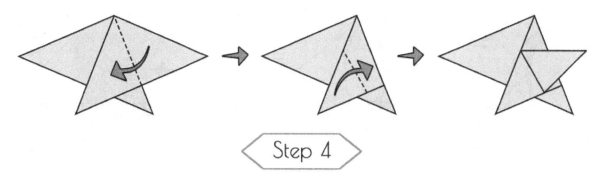

Fold the top layer (right corner) in half so that the two bottom tips overlap. Then fold it up again at an angle so that the top edge ends up horizontal.

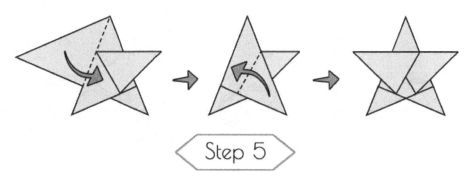

Step 5

Repeat the previous step with the bottom layer (left corner), and turn the figure over.

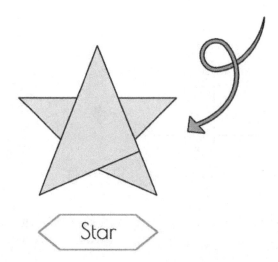

Star

Car

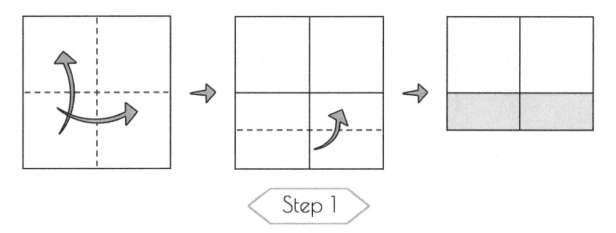

Fold in half lengthwise and crosswise and unfold.
Then fold the bottom edge toward the midline.

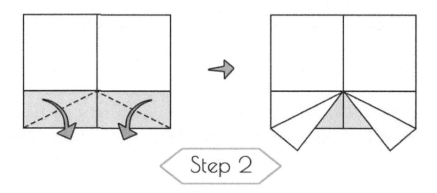

Step 2

Fold down the top corners of the flap you just made.

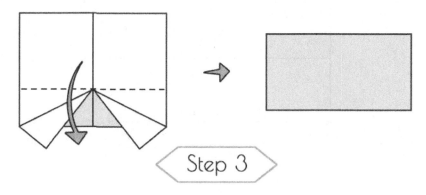

Step 3

Fold the top half of the sheet forward down, covering the lower half.

Car

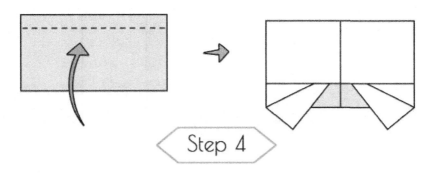

Step 4

Now fold about 3/4 of that same flap back up.

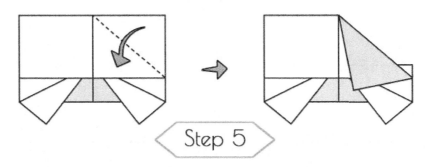

Step 5

Fold the upper right corner down and turn the figure over.

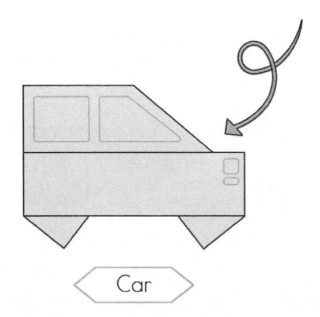

Car

Rocket

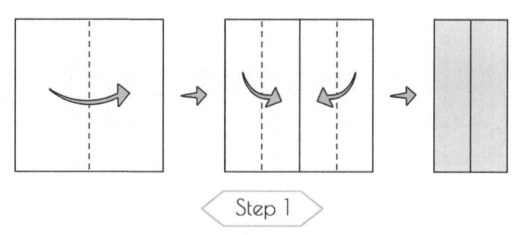

Step 1

Fold in half lengthwise and unfold. Then fold each side again in half inward.

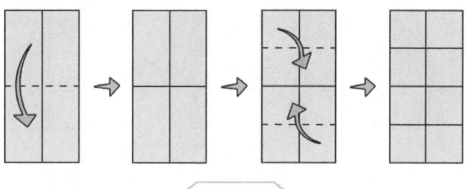

Step 2

Fold in half crosswise and unfold. Then bring the upper and lower edges forward toward the midline and unfold again.

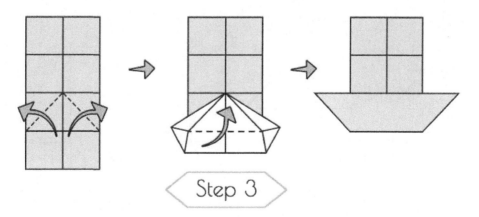

Step 3

From the bottom, fold the second section diagonally outward. As you fold it, the back layer also folds up. Press so that the top edges are horizontal.

Rocket

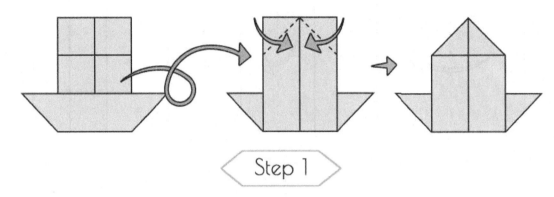

Step 1

Turn the figure over and fold the top corners toward the midline.

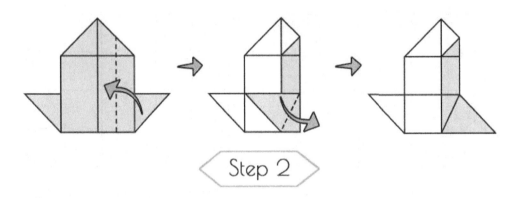

Step 2

Bring the right side to the midline and fold its corner outward at an angle, so that the bottom edge ends up horizontal.

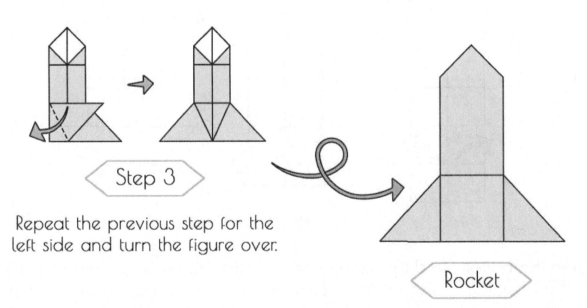

Step 3

Repeat the previous step for the left side and turn the figure over.

Rocket

Shirt

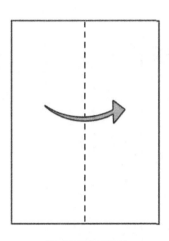

Fold the paper sheet
in half lengthwise
and then unfold it.

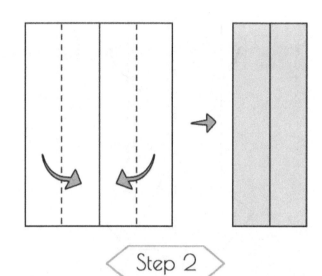

Step 2

Fold each of these halves
again in half lengthwise to get
two flaps and leave them folded.

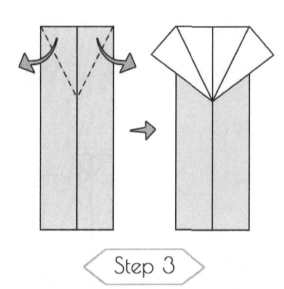

Step 3

Fold the top third of those
flaps outward, at an angle that
forms a V between both flaps.
These are the sleeves of the shirt.

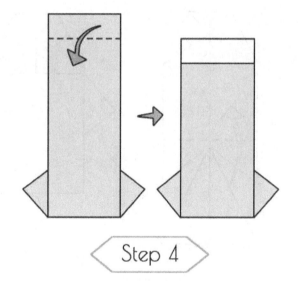

Step 4

Turn the sheet over so that
the V is facing the table. On
the edge opposite the V, fold a 1"
piece of paper down toward you.

Shirt

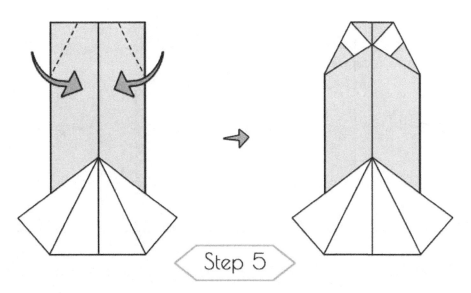

Step 5

Turn the sheet over again, so that the V is back in its original position. Fold the corners of the edge that you folded in the previous step toward the center of the sheet at an angle, so that the two corners touch at the midline. This is the collar of the shirt.

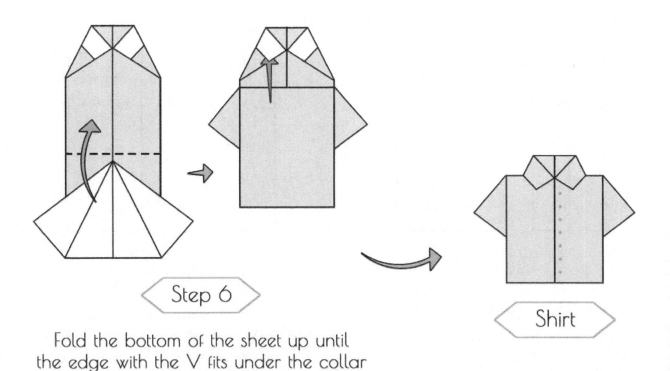

Step 6

Shirt

Fold the bottom of the sheet up until the edge with the V fits under the collar of the shirt and press the bottom edge.

Snake

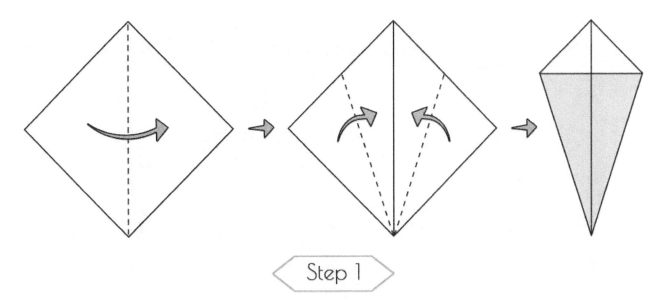

Fold vertically along a diagonal and unfold, then
bring the bottom of the side corners toward the midline.

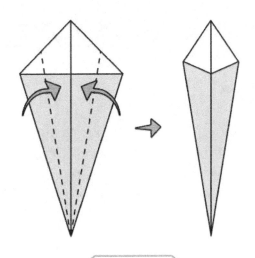

Step 2

Bring the bottom of the side
corners toward the midline again.

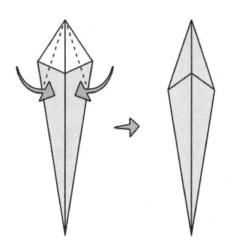

Step 3

Now bring the top of the side
corners toward the midline.

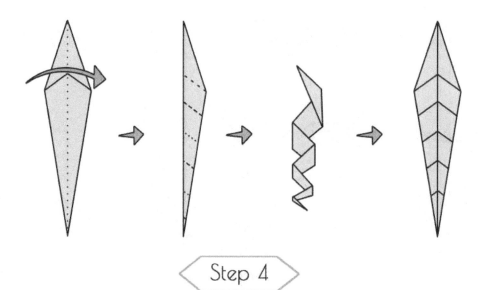

Step 4

Fold back in half and then alternate valley and mountain folds starting at the head and working up to the tail. When you're done, unfold.

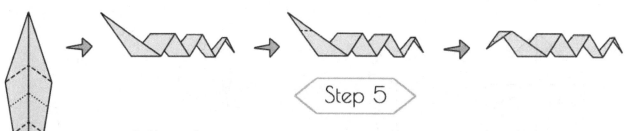

Step 5

Follow the creases you just made, and alternate valley and mountain folds as shown. Then fold the head down with a valley fold and the tip in with a mountain fold.

Snake

Ice Cream

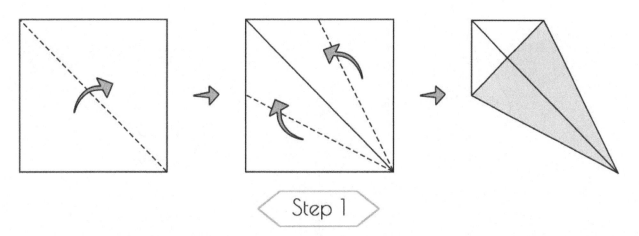

Fold along a diagonal and unfold, then bring the upper right and lower left corners forward to that diagonal.

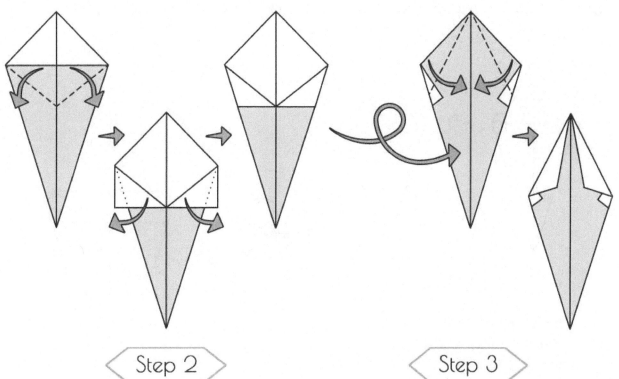

Step 2

Fold both flaps outward at an angle so their bottom edges end up horizontal. Then fold back the tips that stick out from the sides.

Step 3

Turn the figure over and fold the side corners forward toward the midline (without touching it) at an angle.

33

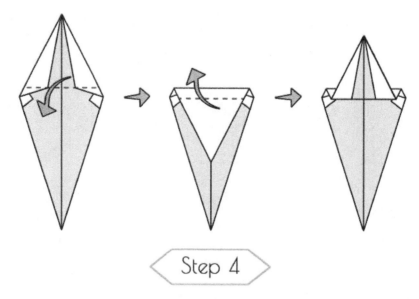

Step 4

Fold the top of the figure down, and then fold it up again.

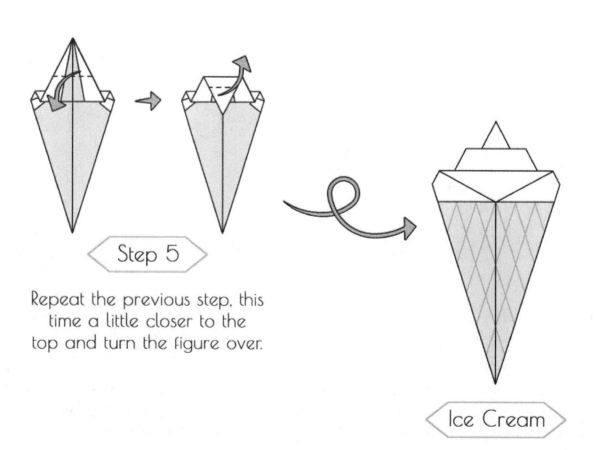

Step 5

Repeat the previous step, this time a little closer to the top and turn the figure over.

Ice Cream

Butterfly

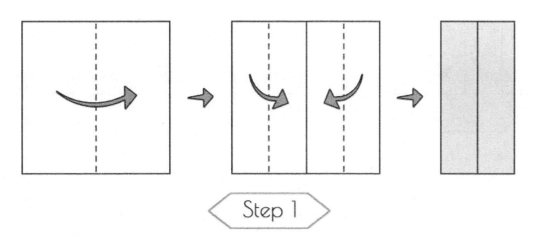

Step 1

Fold in half lengthwise and unfold. Then fold each side again in half inward.

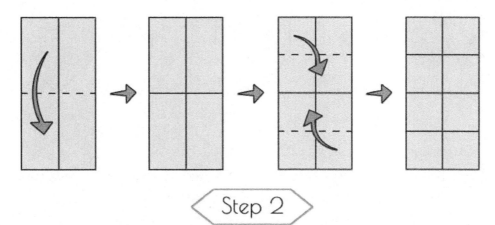

Step 2

Fold in half crosswise and unfold. Then bring the upper and lower edges forward toward the midline and unfold again.

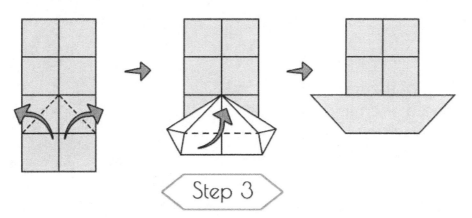

Step 3

From the bottom, fold the second section diagonally outward. As you fold it, the back layer also folds up. Press so that the top edges are horizontal.

Butterfly

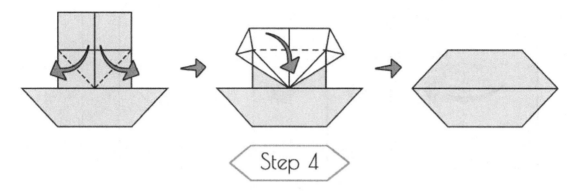

Step 4

Repeat the previous step on the top edge.

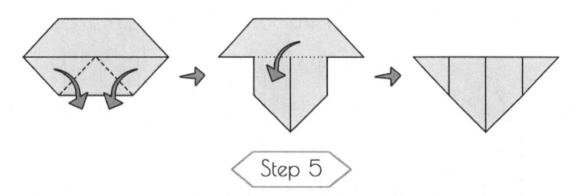

Step 5

Fold the sides of the lower half down toward the midline.
Then fold the top half down towards the back.

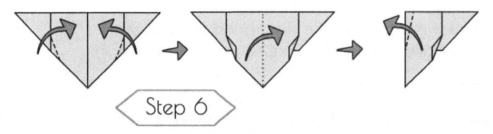

Step 6

Fold the sides of the top layer inward
at a slight angle. Then fold the figure in
half and make a crease in the top half.
Unfold and turn the figure over.

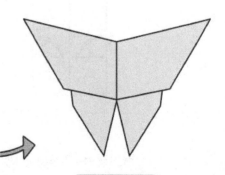

Butterfly

Bat

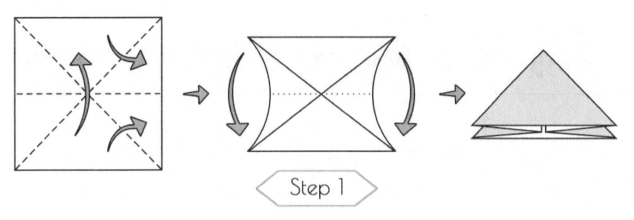

Step 1

Fold in half crosswise and along the two diagonals, and unfold.
Then fold the sides to the center and flatten to get a triangle.

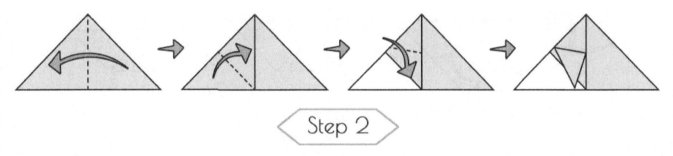

Step 2

Fold the right side of the top layer to the left and fold it again in half up.
Then fold it down at an angle so that only the tip sticks out.

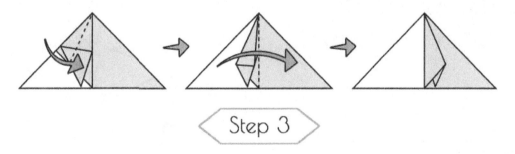

Step 3

Bring the left side to the midline and then fold it all the way to the
right so that the top right layer returns to its starting position.

Bat

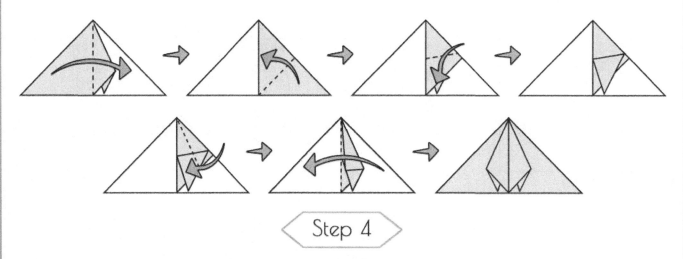

Repeat steps 2 and 3 on the left side.

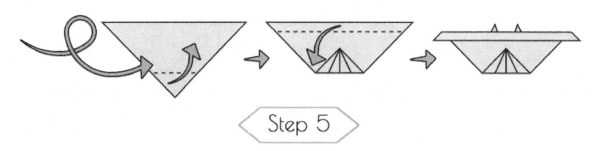

Step 5

Turn the figure over and fold the bottom corner up. Then fold the top edge down (except for the two small tips).

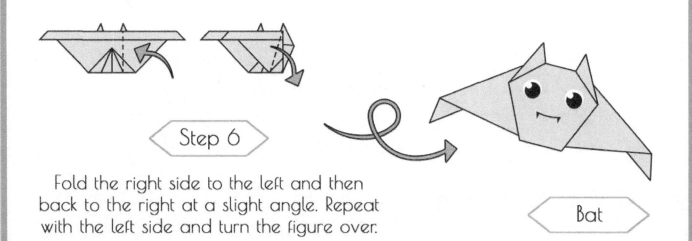

Step 6

Fold the right side to the left and then back to the right at a slight angle. Repeat with the left side and turn the figure over.

Bat

Bookmark

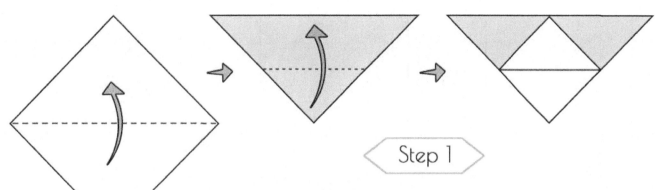

Fold the sheet down along one of its diagonals. Then fold the bottom tip of the top layer only up to the edge.

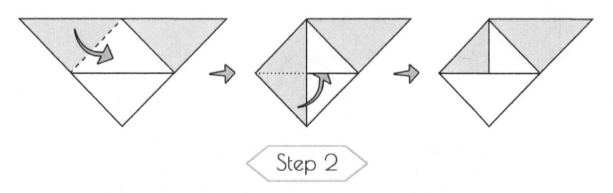

Step 2

Fold the left corner down to the midline. Then fold it up and insert it behind the flap from the previous step.

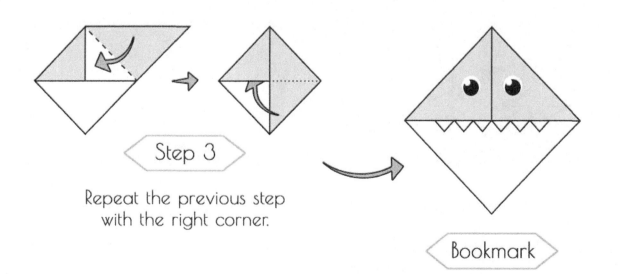

Step 3

Repeat the previous step with the right corner.

Bookmark

39

Whale

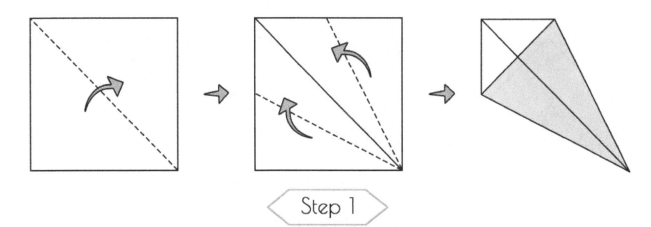

Step 1

Fold along a diagonal and unfold, then bring the upper right and lower left corners forward to that diagonal.

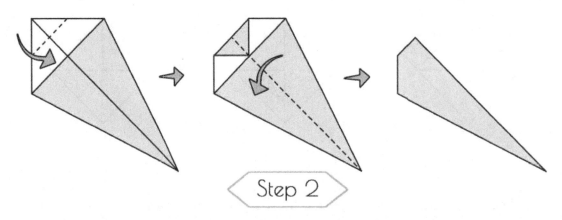

Step 2

Fold the upper left corner forward to the edge of the flaps from the previous step, then fold the figure in half.

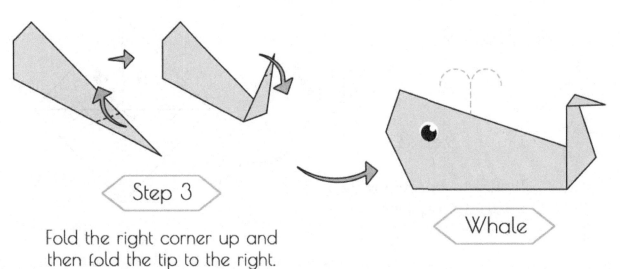

Step 3

Whale

Fold the right corner up and then fold the tip to the right.

40

Dolphin

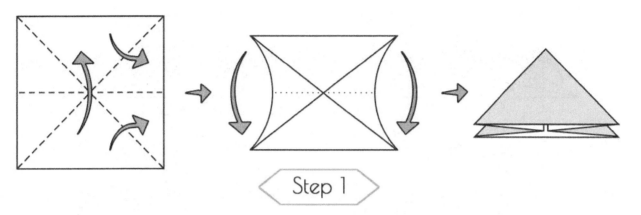

Step 1

Fold in half crosswise and along the two diagonals, and unfold.
Then fold the sides to the center and flatten to get a triangle.

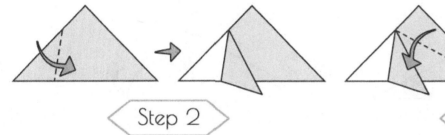

Step 2

Fold the left corner inward
at an angle, so that the tip
sticks out at the bottom edge.

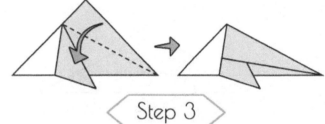

Step 3

Fold the upper right
part down to the
flap you just made.

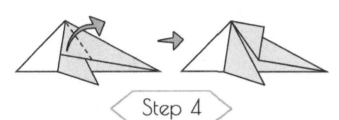

Step 4

Fold up the left side of the
flap from the previous step
so that the tip sticks out.

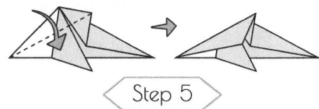

Step 5

Fold the top left part down
to join the left corner and the
tip of the flap you just folded.

41

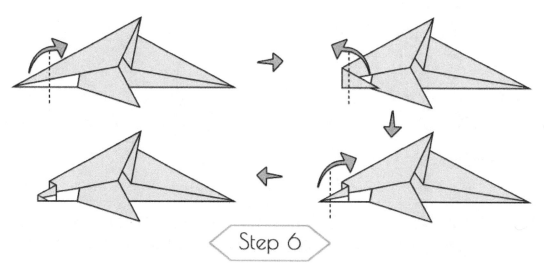

Step 6

Fold the left corner in, then out, and back in to make the dolphin's nose.

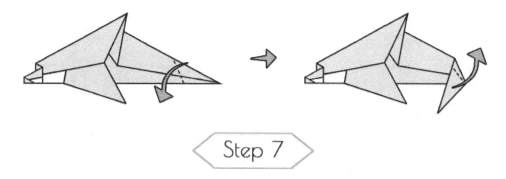

Step 7

Fold the right corner down at an angle so that the tip sticks out at the bottom edge. Now the tricky part: in that tip there are two overlapping layers of paper, leave the inner layer in that position and fold only the top layer up at an angle, then turn the figure over.

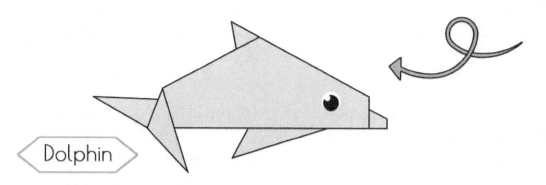

Dolphin

Bird

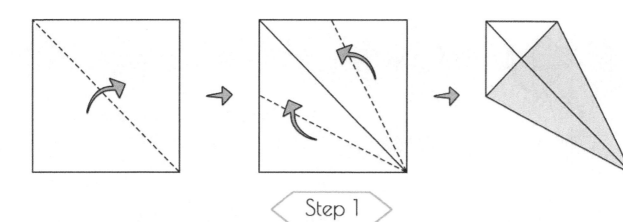

Step 1

Fold along a diagonal and unfold, then bring the upper right and lower left corners forward to that diagonal.

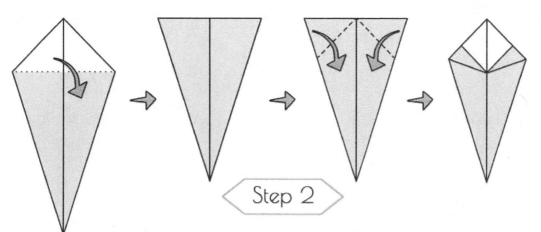

Step 2

Fold the top corner back and then both side corners forward toward the midline.

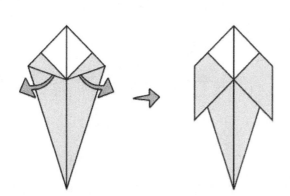

Step 3

The folds from step 1 are just below the flaps from step 2. Unfold them diagonally so that they stick out and point down.

43

Bird

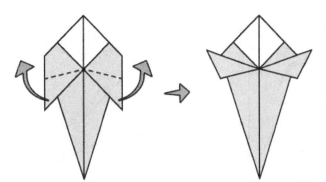

Step 4

Fold the bottom tips of the sides up.

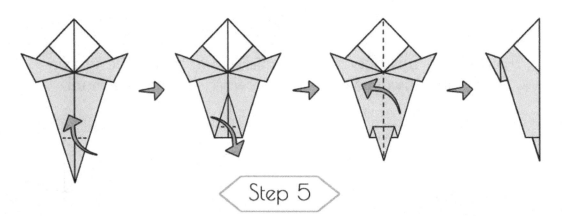

Step 5

Fold the bottom corner up and down again. Then fold the whole figure in half.

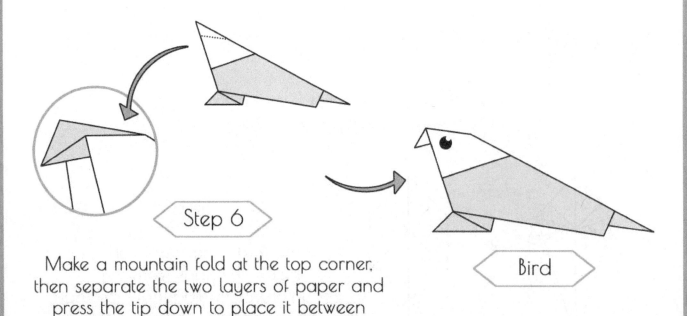

Step 6

Make a mountain fold at the top corner, then separate the two layers of paper and press the tip down to place it between them. This is called an inside reverse fold.

Bird

44

Seal

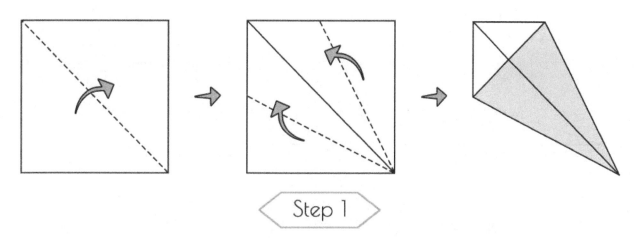

Fold along a diagonal and unfold, then bring the upper right and lower left corners forward to that diagonal.

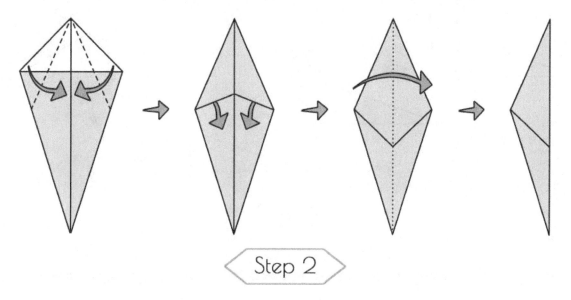

Step 2

Fold the sides down toward the midline. Then unfold the flaps from the previous step that are underneath them, so that they also end up parallel to the midline. Lastly, fold the entire figure in half.

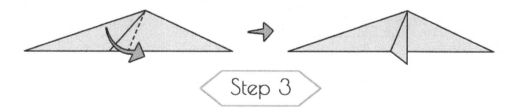

Step 3

Fold the flaps on both sides of the sheet until their edge is vertical.

Seal

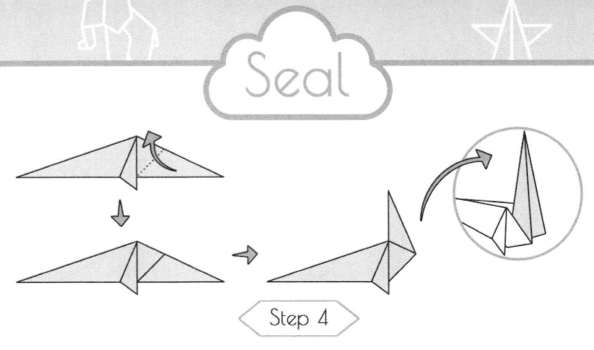

Step 4

Fold the right side up, unfold, and follow that crease to make an inside reverse fold (the fold ends up between both sides of the sheet).

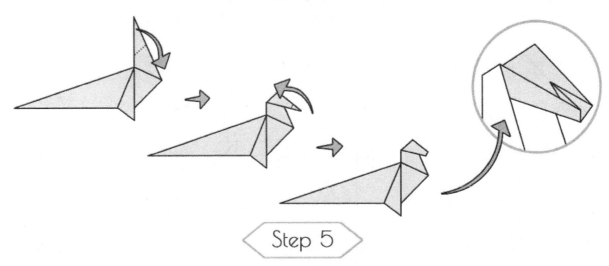

Step 5

Fold that same end down and unfold, then make another inside reverse fold along that crease. Repeat the same step right at the tip.

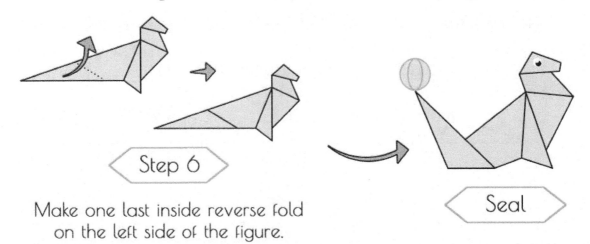

Step 6

Make one last inside reverse fold on the left side of the figure.

Seal

Crane

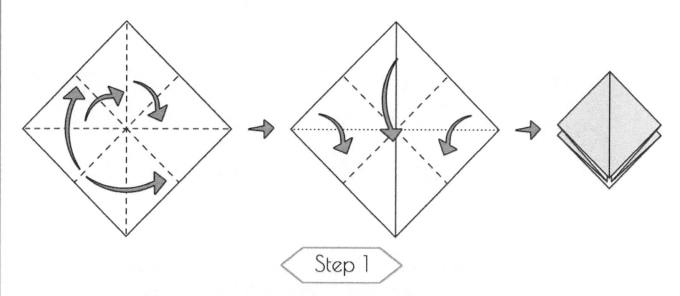

Fold the sheet lengthwise, crosswise and along both diagonals, and unfold. Then fold the top and side corners down and in toward the bottom corner so that the figure collapses into a smaller square.

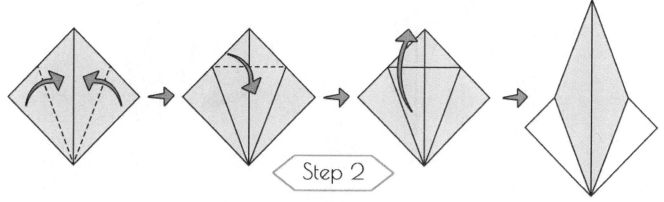

Step 2

Fold the sides toward the midline, the top corner down, and unfold. Then pull the bottom corner all the way up following those creases.

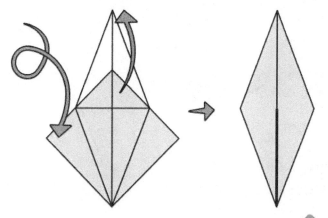

Step 3

Turn the figure over and repeat the previous step on the other side following the same creases. Note that there is an opening in the lower half of the midline.

Crane

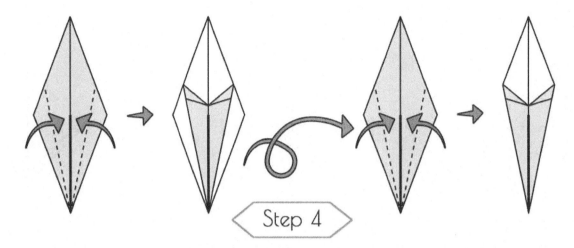

Step 4

Fold the bottom of the sides toward the midline, then turn the figure over and repeat on the other side.

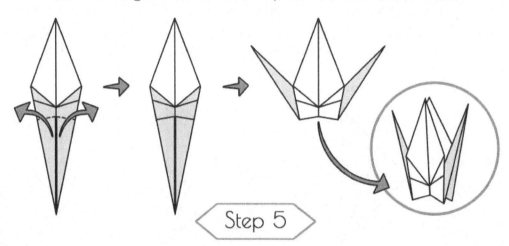

Step 5

Fold the sections on both sides of the opening at a small angle and unfold. Then make an inside reverse fold on them, so that they end up pointing up.

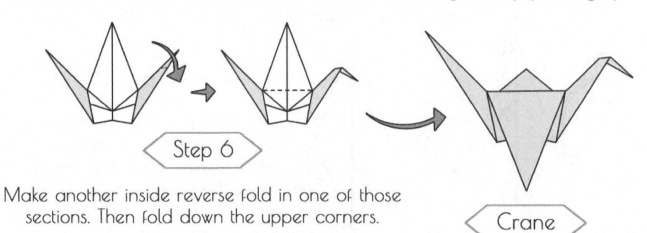

Step 6

Make another inside reverse fold in one of those sections. Then fold down the upper corners.

Crane

Seahorse

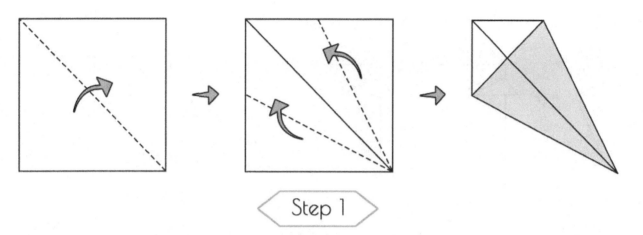

Fold along a diagonal and unfold, then bring the upper right and lower left corners forward to that diagonal.

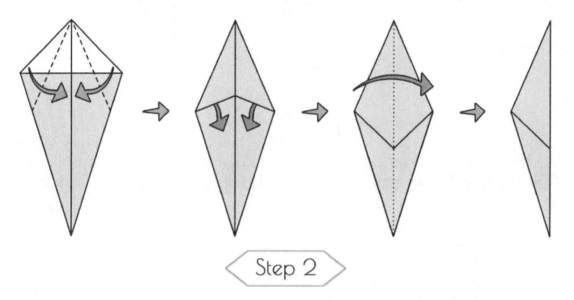

Step 2

Fold the sides down toward the midline. Then unfold the flaps from the previous step that are underneath them, so that they also end up parallel to the midline. Lastly, fold the entire figure in half.

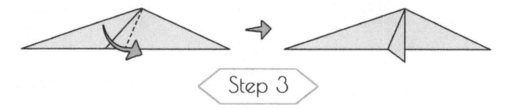

Step 3

Fold the flaps on both sides of the sheet until their edge is vertical.

Seahorse

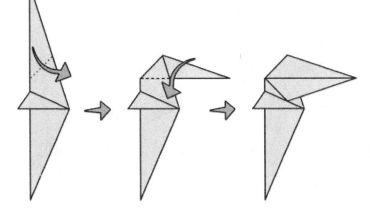

Make an inside reverse fold halfway up the figure, then fold the top layer down to open it.

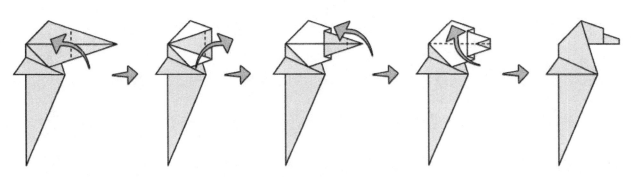

Step 5

Fold the flap you opened in the previous step to the left in half. Now leave a small gap before folding it back to the right and another one to fold it again to the left. Close the reverse fold by folding it up.

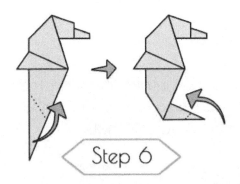

Step 6

Make an inside reverse fold halfway down the figure. Then make a valley fold at the tip and unfold to make a crease, slightly separate the layers of paper and fold them up backward following that crease. This is called an outside reverse fold.

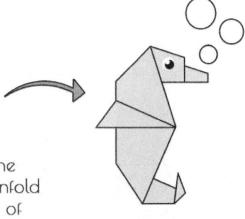

Seahorse

Hummingbird

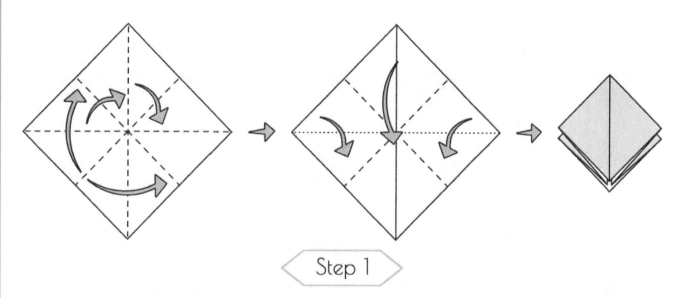

Fold the sheet lengthwise, crosswise and along both diagonals, and unfold. Then fold the top and side corners down and in toward the bottom corner so that the figure collapses into a smaller square.

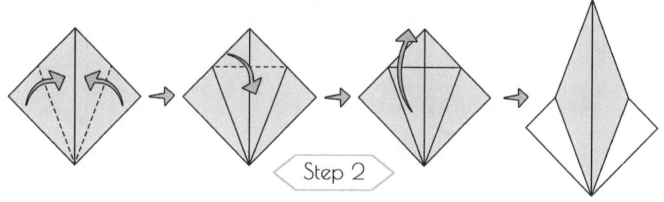

Step 2

Fold the sides toward the midline, the top corner down, and unfold. Then pull the bottom corner all the way up following those creases.

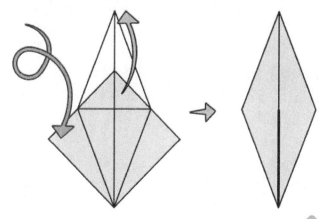

Step 3

Turn the figure over and repeat the previous step on the other side following the same creases. Note that there is an opening in the lower half of the midline.

Hummingbird

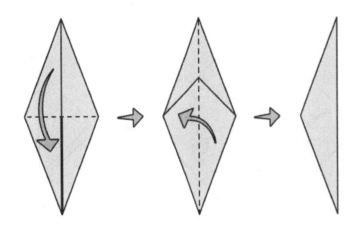

Fold the top layer down in half. Then fold the entire figure in half lengthwise.

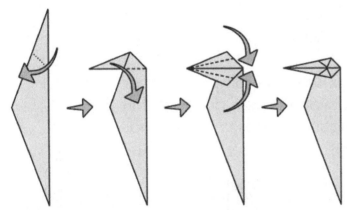

Step 5

Make an inside reverse fold halfway up the figure, and fold the top layer down to open it. Then fold each side in half.

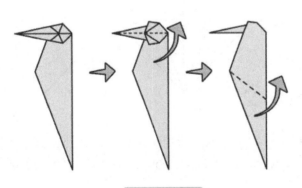

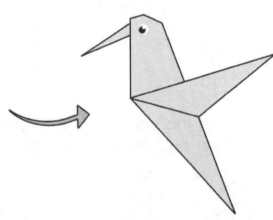

Step 6

When you fold in half in the previous step, you will see that two pockets form on the right side. Pull them out so that they stick out a bit both at the top and the bottom. Then close the inside reverse fold again, and fold the flaps on either side of the lower half of the figure up to the right.

Hummingbird

Lotus Flower

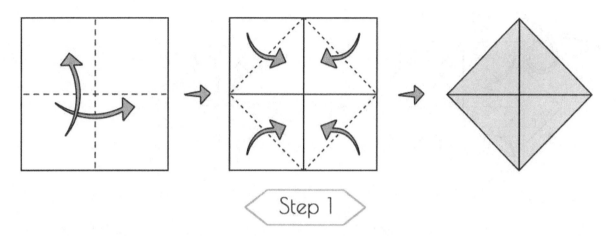

Fold in half lengthwise and crosswise, and unfold.
Then fold all corners toward the center of the sheet.

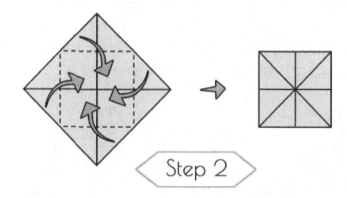

Step 2

Fold all corners toward the center of the sheet again.

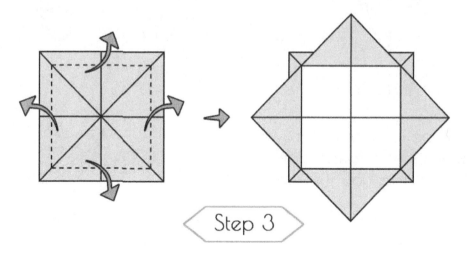

Step 3

Fold the corner tips outward so that they stick out a little from the sides.

53

Lotus Flower

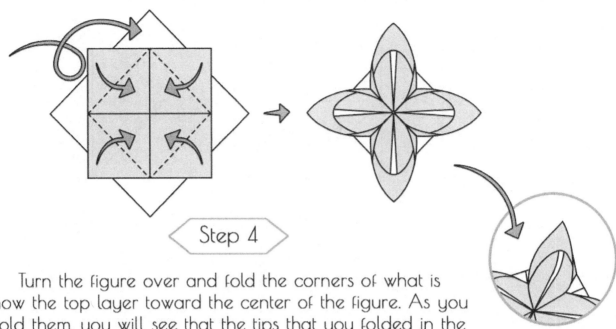

Turn the figure over and fold the corners of what is now the top layer toward the center of the figure. As you fold them, you will see that the tips that you folded in the previous step lift up, so once they are vertical give them a rounded shape so that they look like petals.

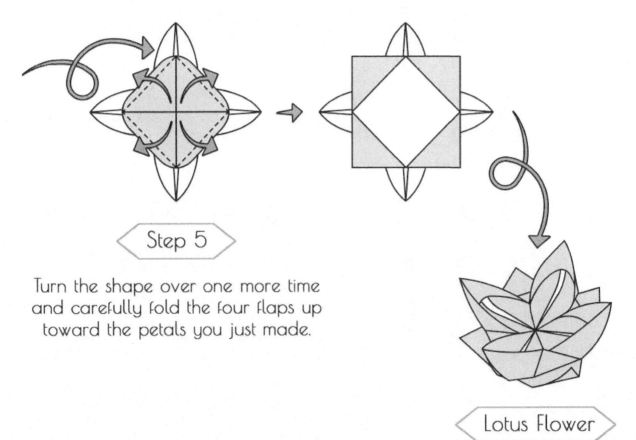

Step 5

Turn the shape over one more time and carefully fold the four flaps up toward the petals you just made.

Lotus Flower

Brachiosaurus

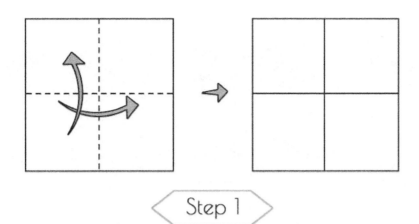

Step 1

Fold in half lengthwise and crosswise, and unfold.

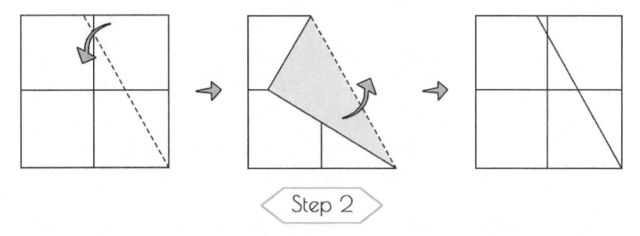

Step 2

Bring the upper right corner to the left side of the horizontal crease and unfold.

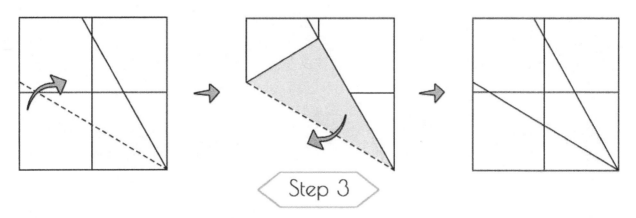

Step 3

Bring the lower left corner to the upper side of the vertical crease and unfold.

Brachiosaurus

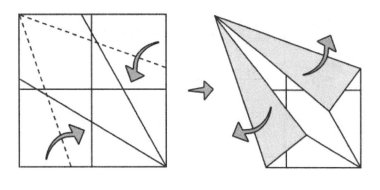

Starting now from the upper left corner, bring the upper right and lower left corners toward the creases from steps 2 and 3, and unfold.

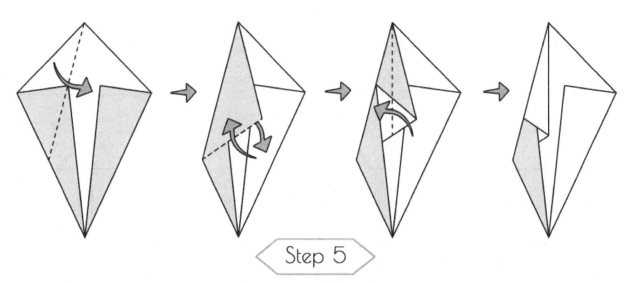

Step 5

Turn the figure a little and fold the upper left side inward along the crease from step 2. Then unfold the layer that is immediately below and fold it up following the same edge that you just made. Lastly, fold that entire section in half outward.

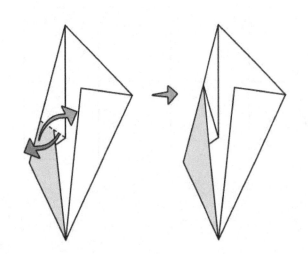

Step 6

Unfold the layer immediately below again and fold it up the edge of the top layer, so the tip is now on top but still in the same position.

Brachiosaurus

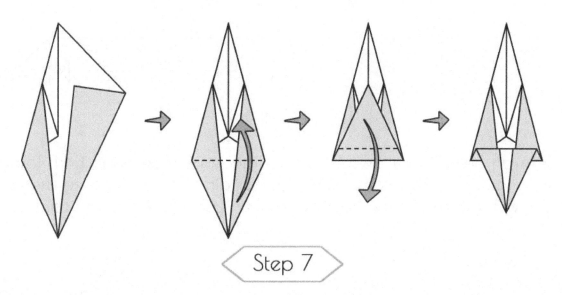

Step 7

Repeat steps 5 and 6 on the right side of the figure. Then fold the bottom corner up and down again, leaving a small space between the two folds.

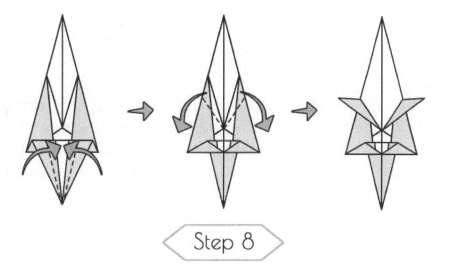

Step 8

Fold the sides of the lower section toward the midline. As you do so, you will see that the corners separate from the bottom layer; flatten them into a triangle shape. Then fold the side flaps outward so they stick out the sides.

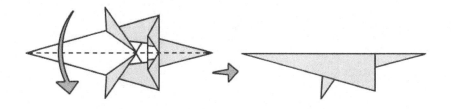

Step 9

Rotate the figure to the left and fold it in half.

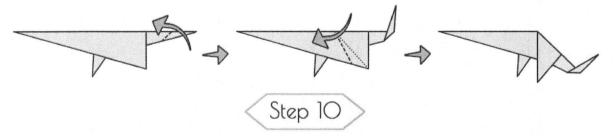

Make an outside reverse fold at the right end. Then bring both lower tips to the left with a valley and a mountain fold so that they overlap with the rest of the figure and their edge ends up vertical.

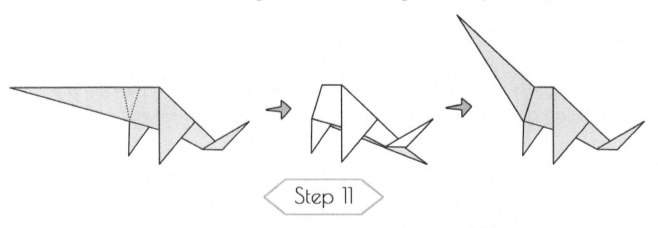

Make two inside reverse folds in a row: the first (right dotted line) will make the left end of the figure face down between the two layers of paper, the second (left dotted line, can't be seen in the middle step) will make that end point up and left at an angle.

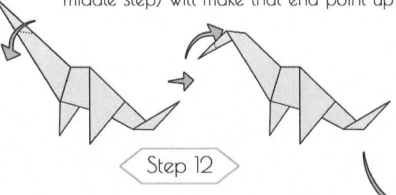

Make two inside reverse folds at the tip of the upper left corner, the first downward and the second upward.

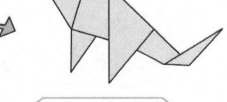

Brachiosaurus

Elephant

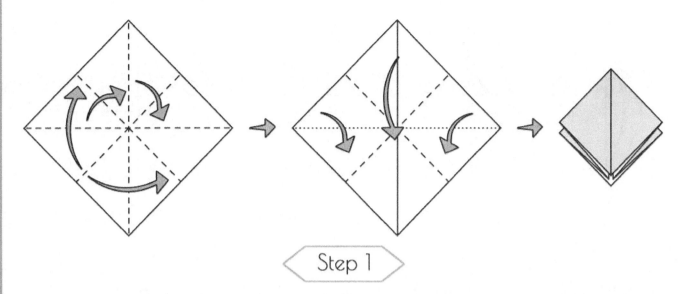

Step 1

Fold the sheet lengthwise, crosswise and along both diagonals, and unfold. Then fold the top and side corners down and in toward the bottom corner so that the figure collapses into a smaller square.

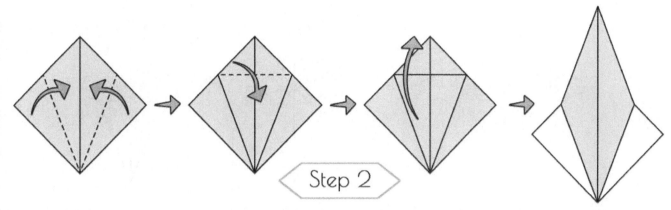

Step 2

Fold the sides toward the midline, the top corner down, and unfold. Then pull the bottom corner all the way up following those creases.

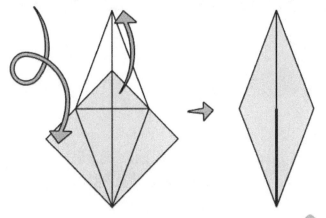

Step 3

Turn the figure over and repeat the previous step on the other side following the same creases. Note that there is an opening in the lower half of the midline.

Elephant

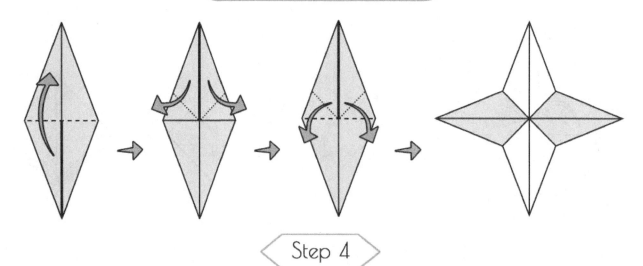

Fold the bottom section with the opening up, then fold each side diagonally outward and unfold. Each side piece has two layers of paper, use those creases you just made to unfold them down and press.

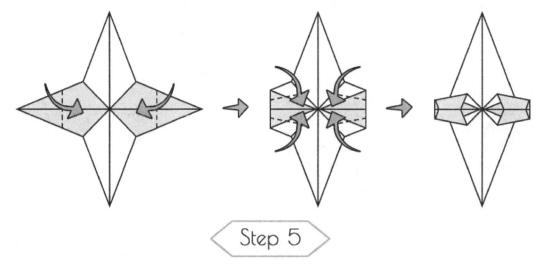

Fold the sides in half toward the center. Then bring their edges to the midline.

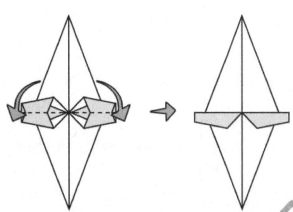

Fold both side pieces down in half. These are the front legs.

Elephant

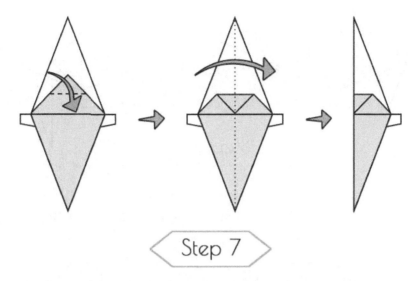

Turn the figure over and fold the tip in its center down in half. Then fold the entire figure in half.

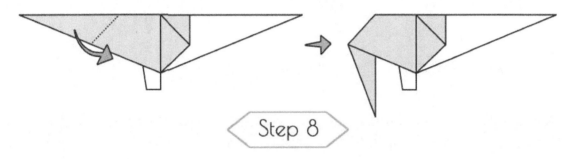

Rotate the figure to the right. Make an inside reverse fold at the left end so that its right edge ends up vertical.

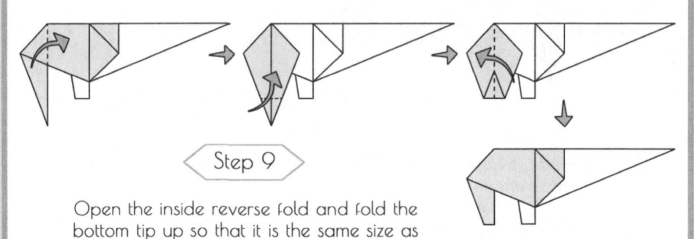

Open the inside reverse fold and fold the bottom tip up so that it is the same size as the front legs. Then close the fold again.

Elephant

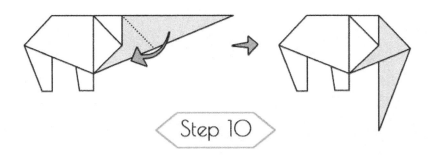

Make an inside reverse fold at the right
end so that its left edge ends up vertical.

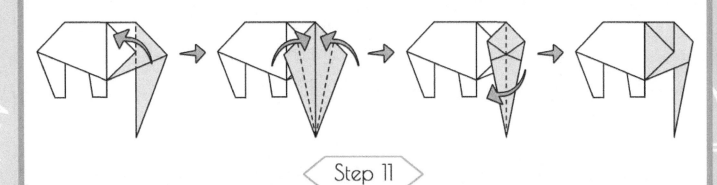

Step 11

Open the inside reverse fold and fold its side edges toward the
midline. Then close the fold again. This is the elephant's trunk.

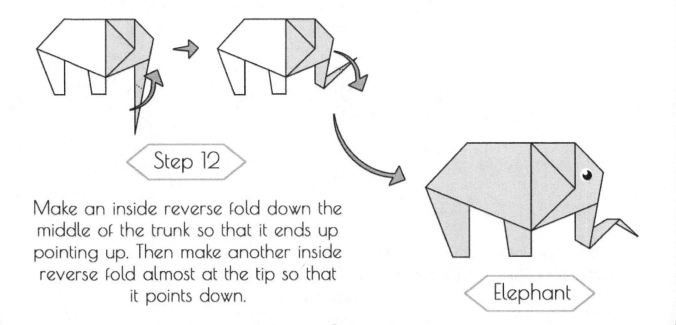

Step 12

Make an inside reverse fold down the
middle of the trunk so that it ends up
pointing up. Then make another inside
reverse fold almost at the tip so that
it points down.

Elephant

Dragon

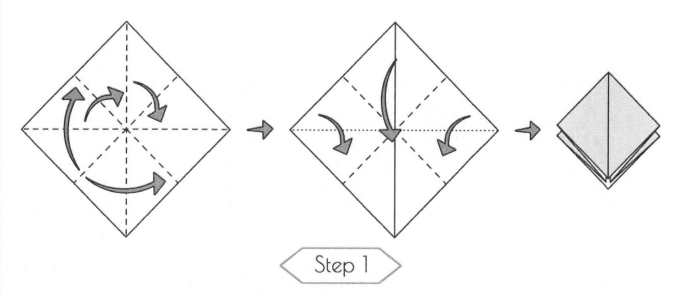

Step 1

Fold the sheet lengthwise, crosswise and along both diagonals, and unfold. Then fold the top and side corners down and in toward the bottom corner so that the figure collapses into a smaller square.

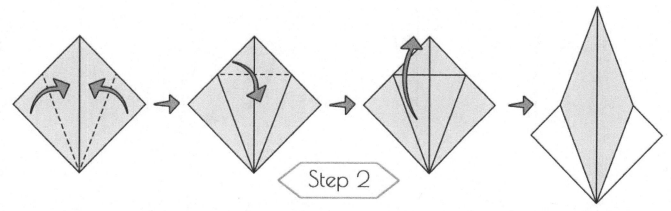

Step 2

Fold the sides toward the midline, the top corner down, and unfold. Then pull the bottom corner all the way up following those creases.

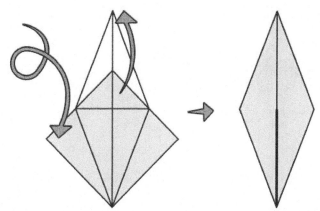

Step 3

Turn the figure over and repeat the previous step on the other side following the same creases. Note that there is an opening in the lower half of the midline.

Dragon

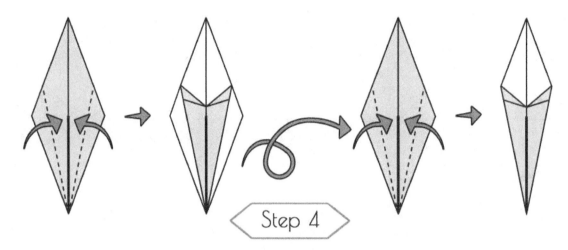

Step 4

Fold the bottom of the sides toward the midline, then
turn the figure over and repeat on the other side.

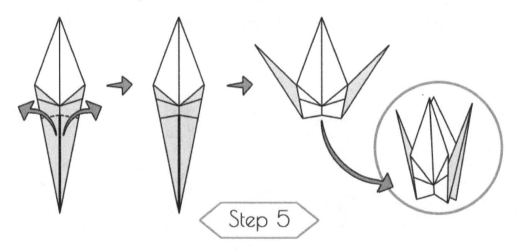

Step 5

Fold the sections on both sides of the opening at a small angle and unfold.
Then make an inside reverse fold on them, so that they end up pointing up.

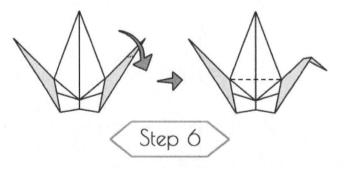

Step 6

Make an inside reverse fold toward the tip of one of those sections.

Dragon

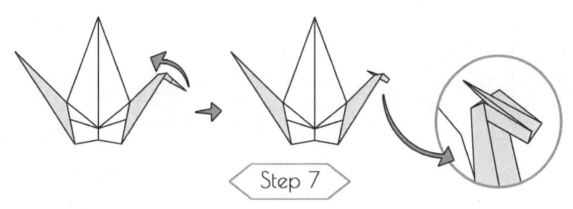

Step 7

Make another inside reverse fold at that end, so that it sticks out at the top.

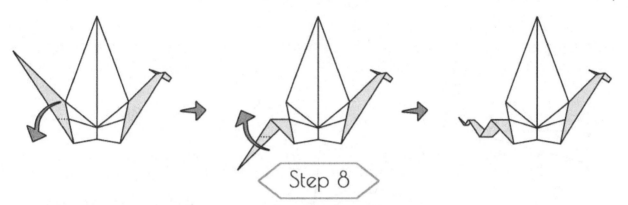

Step 8

Make an inside reverse fold on the opposite section so that it points down. Then make another inside reverse fold so that it points up and keep repeating this movement until the entire section is folded.

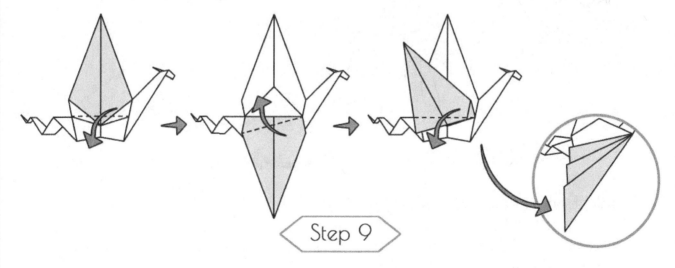

Step 9

Fold the top corner horizontally down, then up at an angle and back down horizontally. Keep folding up and down like this until the entire section is folded.

Dragon

Step 10

Turn the figure over and repeat step 9 with the top corner on the other side.

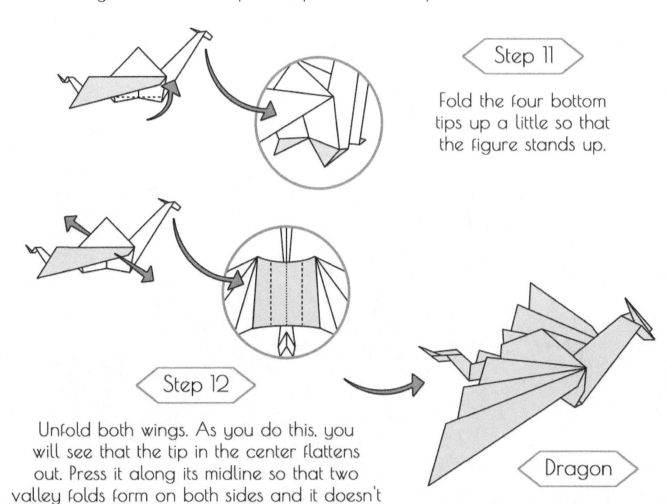

Step 11

Fold the four bottom tips up a little so that the figure stands up.

Step 12

Unfold both wings. As you do this, you will see that the tip in the center flattens out. Press it along its midline so that two valley folds form on both sides and it doesn't stick out as much (see top view zoom).

Dragon

Pop-it Toy

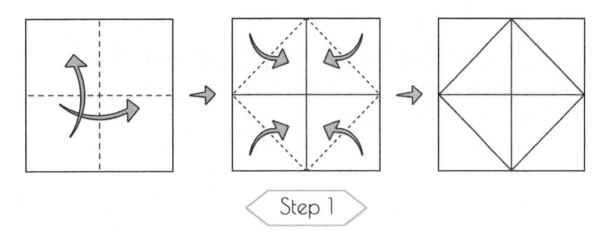

Fold in half lengthwise and crosswise, and unfold. Then fold all corners toward the center of the sheet and unfold again.

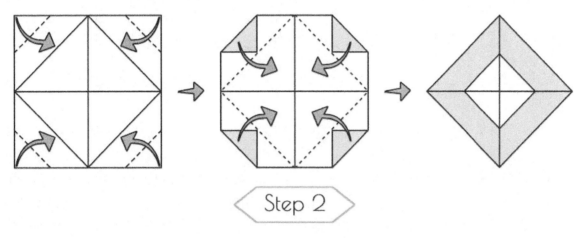

Step 2

Fold the corners inward toward the diagonal creases from the previous step. Then fold inward again along those creases.

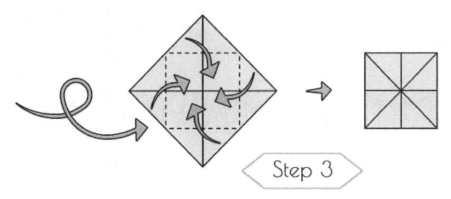

Step 3

Turn the figure over and fold all corners toward the center of the sheet.

Pop-it Toy

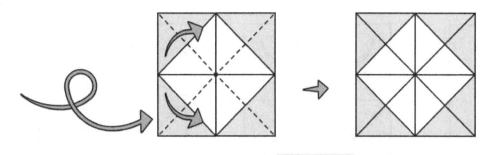

Step 4

Turn the figure over and fold along both diagonals, then unfold.

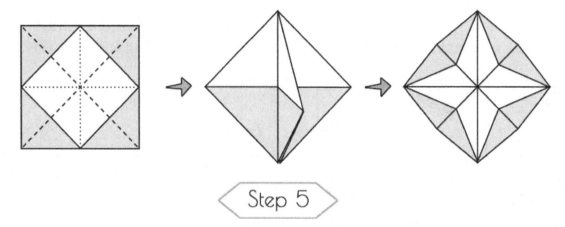

Step 5

Make mountain folds along the vertical and horizontal creases, and valley folds along the diagonals to collapse the figure. Then open those folds a bit, but without returning to its flat position to make it look three-dimensional.

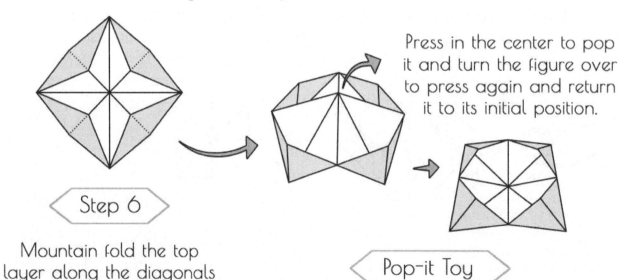

Press in the center to pop it and turn the figure over to press again and return it to its initial position.

Step 6

Mountain fold the top layer along the diagonals to form a pocket.

Pop-it Toy

Fish

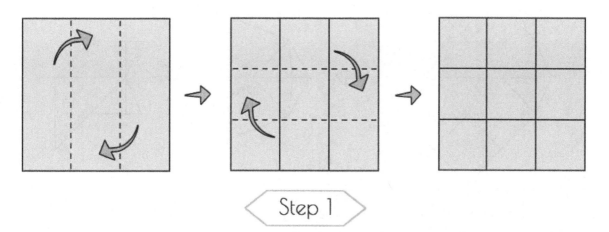

Step 1

Fold the sheet in three equal parts lengthwise and crosswise, then unfold.

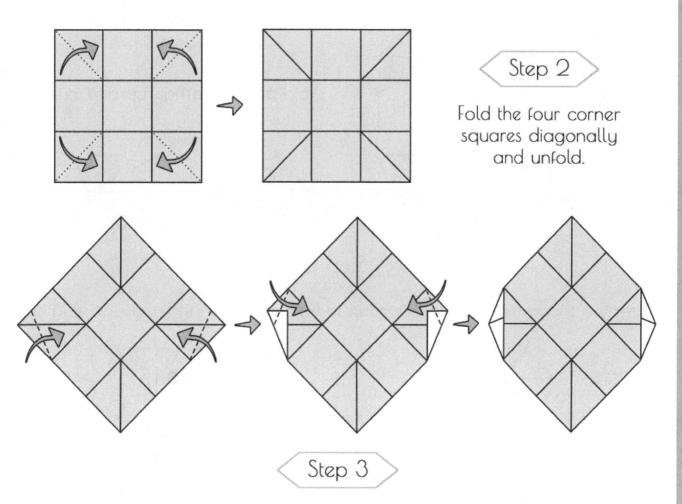

Step 2

Fold the four corner squares diagonally and unfold.

Step 3

Turn the sheet to the side and fold the bottom of the side corners up until their edge is vertical. Repeat with the top of both side corners.

Fish

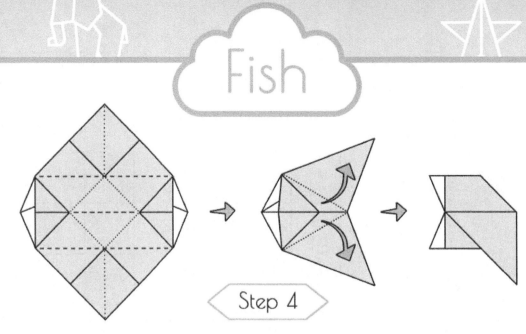

Step 4

Make mountain and valley folds carefully as shown in the figure (there are no arrows to show all lines more clearly). Then fold the flaps that form at the top and bottom, turn vertically and flatten the figure.

Step 5

Fold the flap in half up and in.

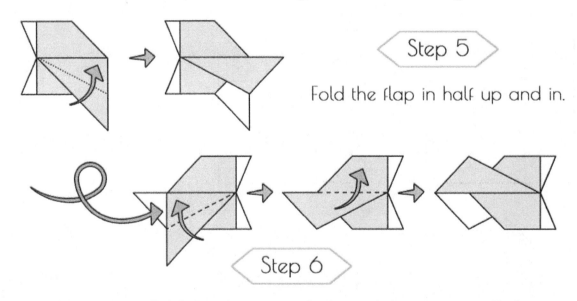

Step 6

Turn the shape over. Fold the flap up in half and then again all the way up.

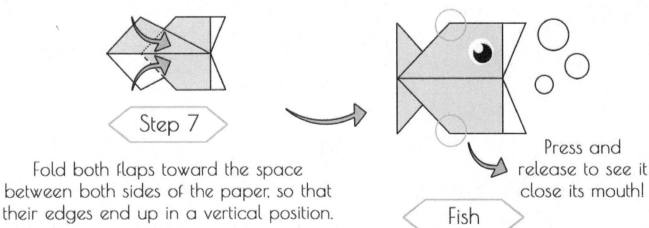

Step 7

Fold both flaps toward the space between both sides of the paper, so that their edges end up in a vertical position.

Press and release to see it close its mouth!

Fish

Peacock

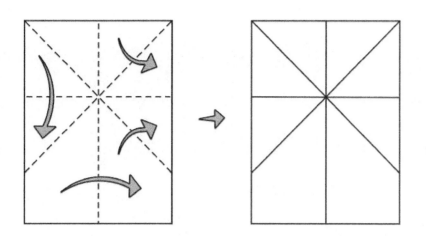

Fold both top corners diagonally, then fold vertically and horizontally at the point where those creases meet, and unfold.

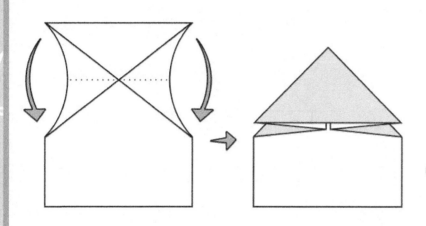

Step 2

Fold the sides to the center and flatten to get a triangle with a piece of paper left unfolded (the longer this piece, the bigger the tail will be).

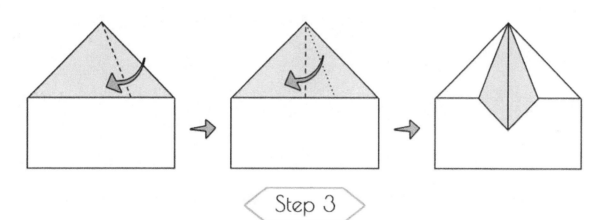

Step 3

Fold the top right side toward the midline and unfold. Then unfold the two layers of that section following that crease and flatten.

Peacock

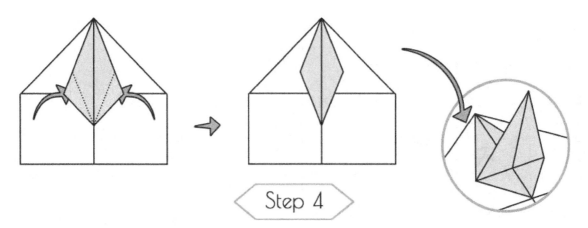

Fold the sides in toward the midline, so that the upper edge ends up being horizontal. Check the 3D view to see how it should look if you fold the bottom tip up (not part of the process though).

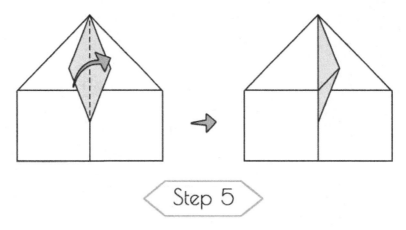

Step 5

Fold that section in half to the right.

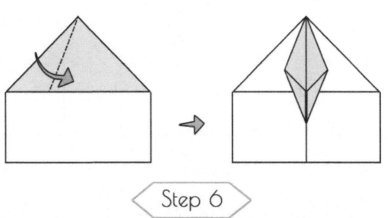

Step 6

Repeat steps 3 through 5 on the top left side. Note that there is an opening between the lower sections.

Peacock

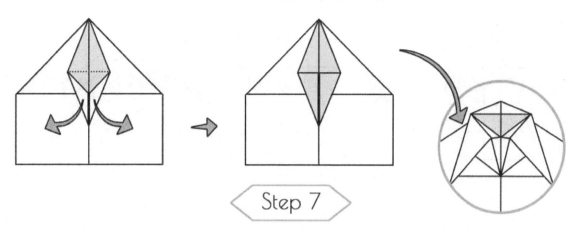

Pull the bottom sections to the sides to open a gap between them and insert the tip that is above them inward and upward.

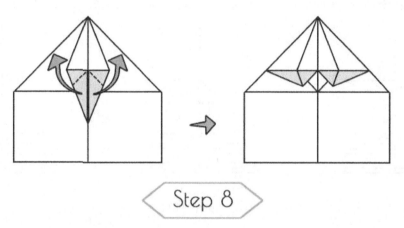

Step 8

Make an inside reverse fold on the bottom sections so that the top edge ends up horizontal.

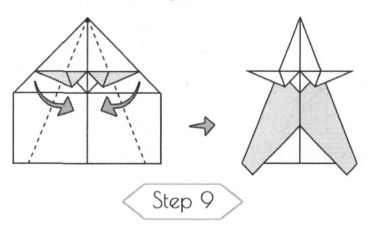

Step 9

Bring the top of the bottom layer toward the midline, but behind the section you've been folding so far.

Peacock

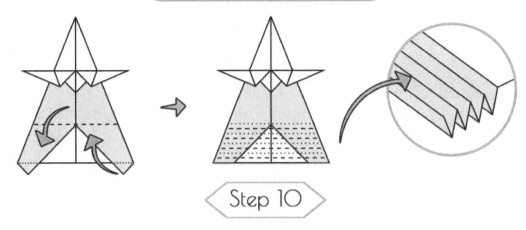

Fold back the tips that stick out the bottom edge, then fold the figure horizontally where the two flaps touch, and unfold. With that crease as the limit, fold the lower part in an accordion shape, alternating valley and mountain folds.

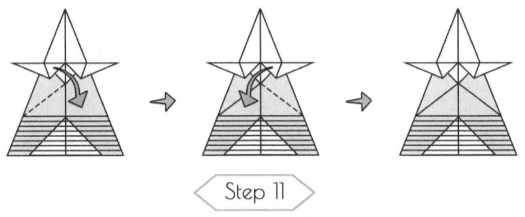

Step 11

Fold the top corner diagonally to the right toward the crease from the previous step and unfold. Then repeat to the left and unfold again.

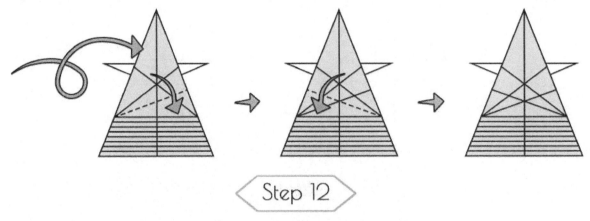

Step 12

Turn the figure over and fold in the same way as in the previous step, but at a slightly smaller angle.

Peacock

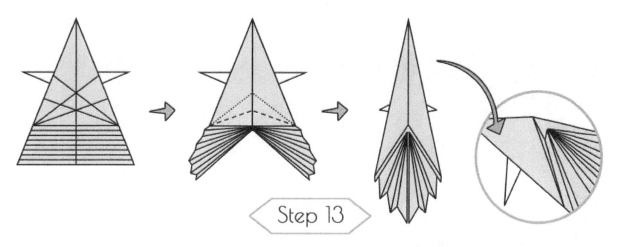

This is the trickiest step: fold the entire accordion section in half, as you form a triangle between the creases from steps 11 and 12. You will see that the figure folds in half lengthwise as you make that triangle. This way, the base of the tail ends up hidden between the two sides of the sheet.

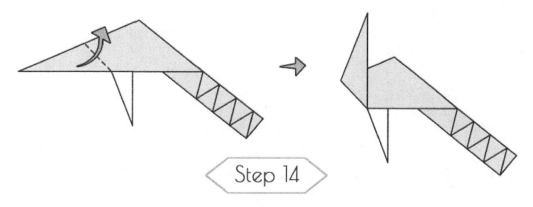

Step 14

Turn the figure to the side and flatten. Then make an outside reverse fold on the opposite end of the tail, so that it ends up vertical.

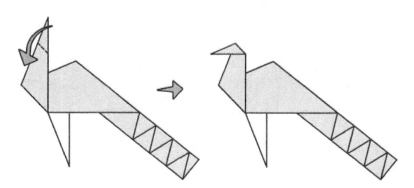

Step 15

Make another outside reverse fold at the tip of that section.

Peacock

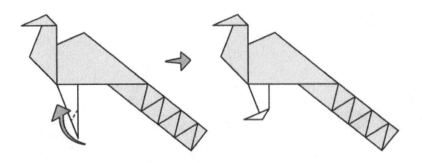

Step 16

Make outside reverse folds on the two sections that are pointing down.

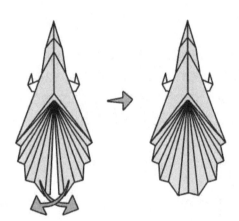

Step 17

To be sure that the tail won't open along its center opening, place the first fold on one side over the first one on the other side and fold them in half all along their back.

Press carefully here to see the peacock's tail lift up and open.

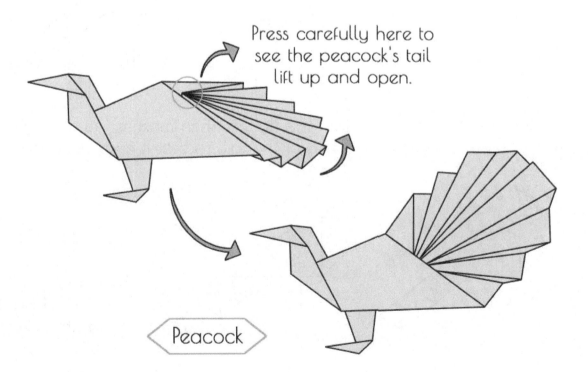

Peacock

Frog

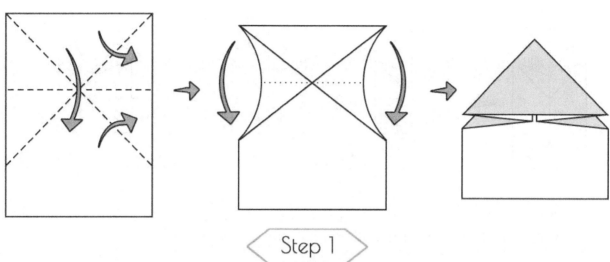

Step 1

Fold both top corners diagonally until they reach the opposite edge of the sheet, then fold horizontally at the point where those diagonals meet, and unfold. Then fold the sides to the center and flatten to get a triangle with a piece of paper left unfolded.

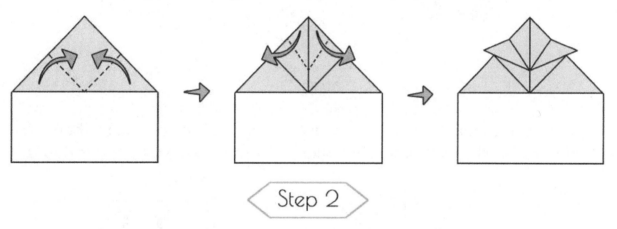

Step 2

Fold the sides of the top layer up in half. Then fold them back down at an angle so that the tips stick out of the sides of the figure.

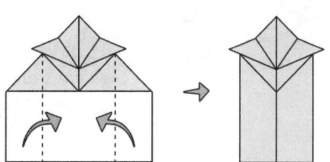

Step 3

Fold the sides of the bottom layer in toward the midline.

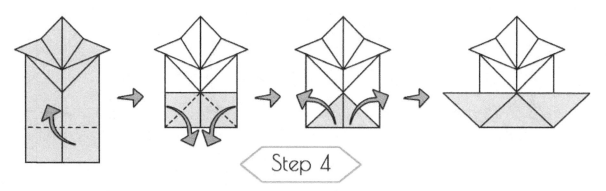

Step 4

Fold the bottom of the figure up in half and its corners back down diagonally. Then pull those flaps sideways to unfold them and press.

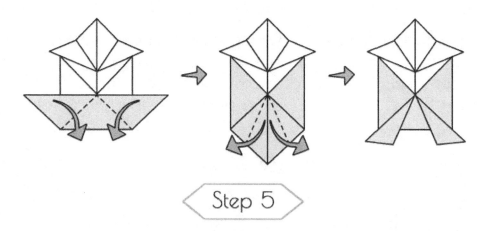

Step 5

Fold the sides down along the creases from the previous step. Then fold them up slightly so that the tips stick out from both sides of the figure.

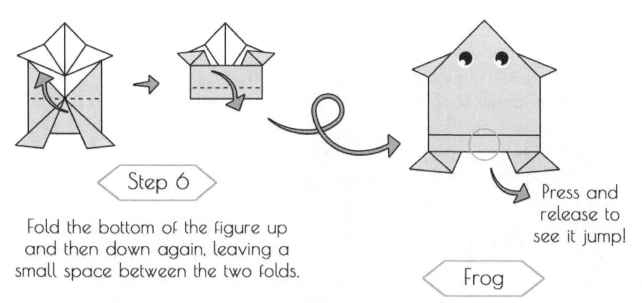

Step 6

Fold the bottom of the figure up and then down again, leaving a small space between the two folds.

Press and release to see it jump!

Frog

Tulip

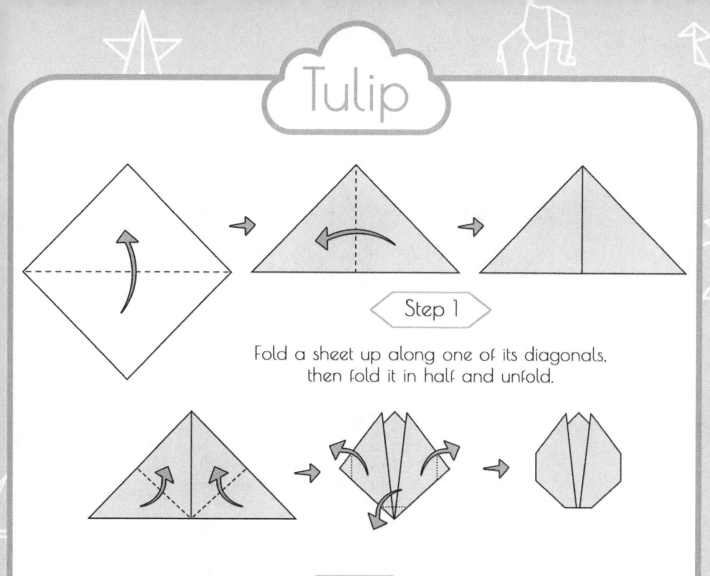

Step 1

Fold a sheet up along one of its diagonals, then fold it in half and unfold.

Step 2

Fold both side corners up so they stick out on both sides of the top tip. Then fold the side and bottom tips back and the flower is ready.

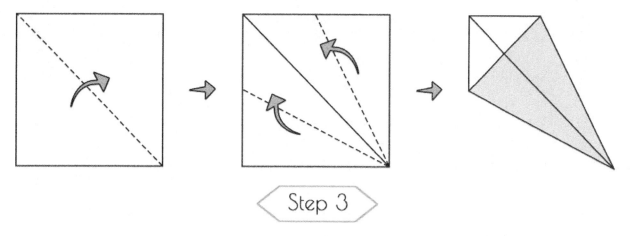

Step 3

Take another sheet, fold along a diagonal, and unfold. Then bring the upper right and lower left corners forward to that diagonal.

Tulip

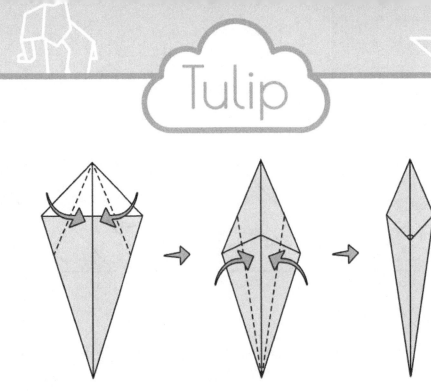

Fold the sides down towards the midline
and then back up again in the same way.

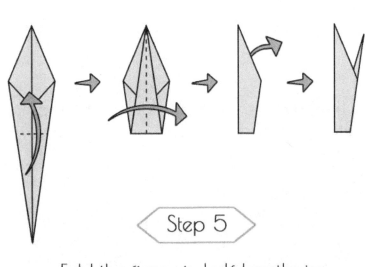

Fold the figure in half lengthwise
and then widthwise. Angle the tip
that remains on the inside of the
fold outward and the stem is done.

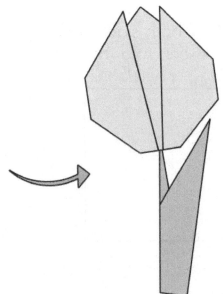

Tulip

Koala

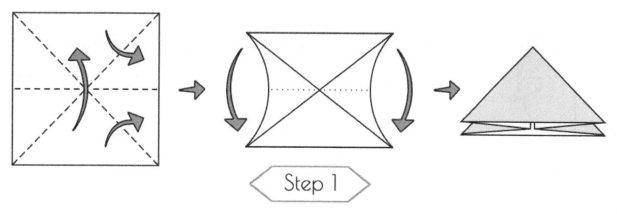

Step 1

Fold in half crosswise and along the two diagonals, and unfold. Then fold both sides in toward the center and press the edges to make a triangle.

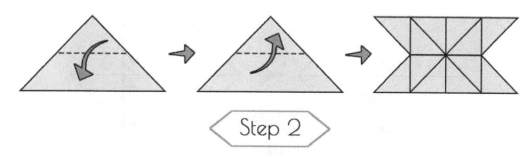

Step 2

Fold the figure in half and unfold. Then fold the top layer up along that crease and the flaps that are between the two layers will also move up. Flatten the entire figure, including those inside flaps.

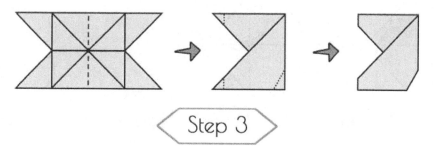

Step 3

Fold the figure in half to the left. Then make inside reverse folds in all the left corners and in the lower right corner.

Koala

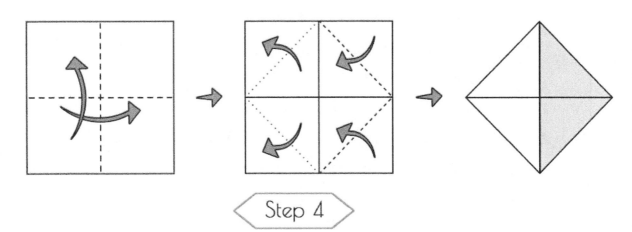

Step 4

Fold another sheet in half lengthwise and crosswise, and unfold. Then fold the two left corners backward and the two right corners forward.

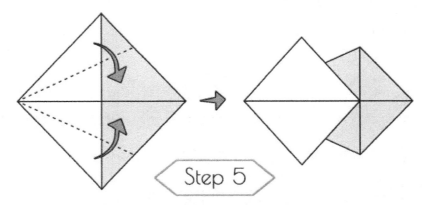

Step 5

Bring the top and bottom corners to the midline and press the edges. You will see the corners that we folded backward sticking out from the sides.

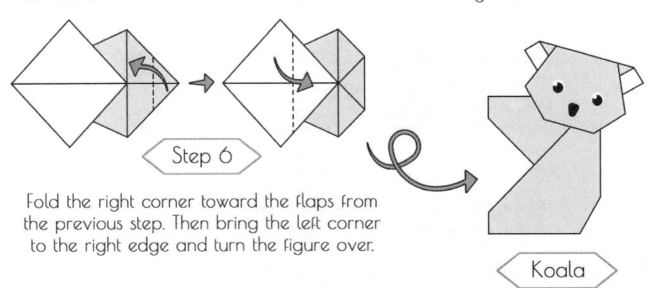

Step 6

Fold the right corner toward the flaps from the previous step. Then bring the left corner to the right edge and turn the figure over.

Koala

Carrot

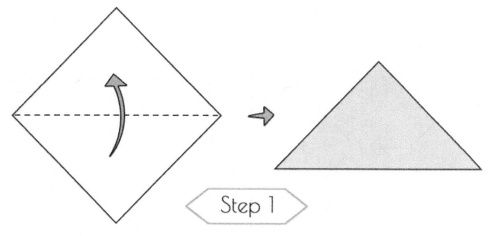

Step 1

Fold a sheet up along one of its diagonals.

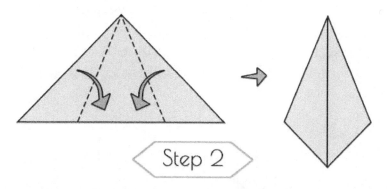

Step 2

Fold both side corners down towards the midline.

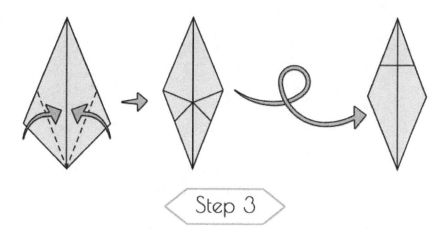

Step 3

Fold both side corners up towards the midline, then turn the figure over.
This is the body of the carrot.

Carrot

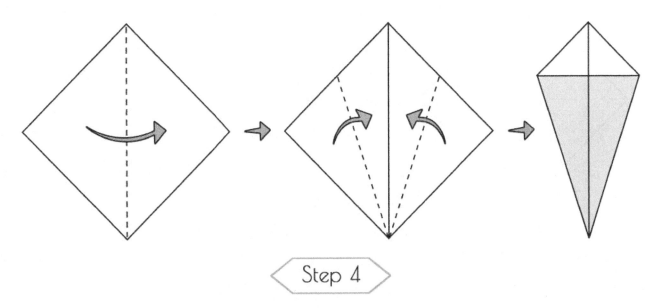

Step 4

Take a sheet smaller than the previous one. Fold vertically along a diagonal and unfold, then bring the bottom of the side corners toward the midline.

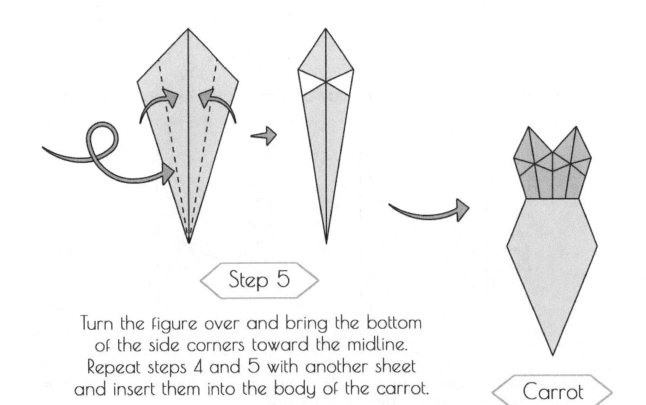

Step 5

Turn the figure over and bring the bottom of the side corners toward the midline. Repeat steps 4 and 5 with another sheet and insert them into the body of the carrot.

Carrot

Box

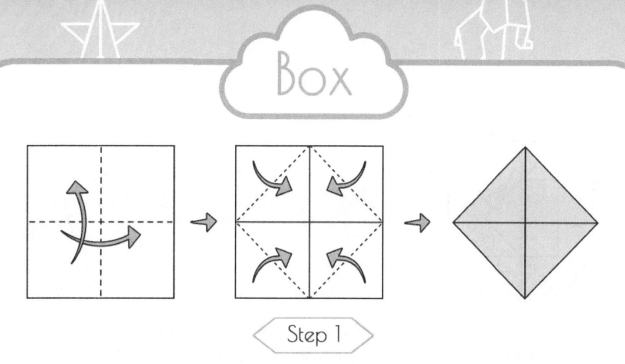

Step 1

Fold in half lengthwise and crosswise, and unfold. Then fold all corners toward the center of the sheet. Repeat with a slightly larger sheet.

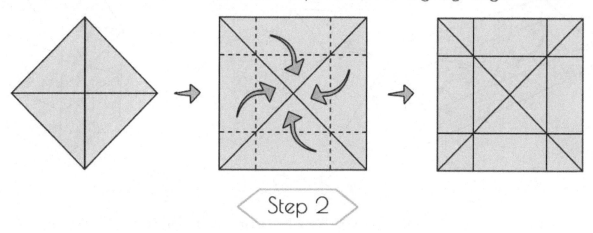

Step 2

Rotate the figure a little to the side. Then fold all the edges forward toward the center of the sheet and unfold. Repeat on the other sheet.

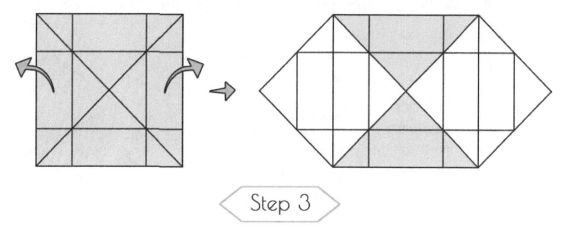

Step 3

Unfold the side corners. Repeat on the other sheet.

Box

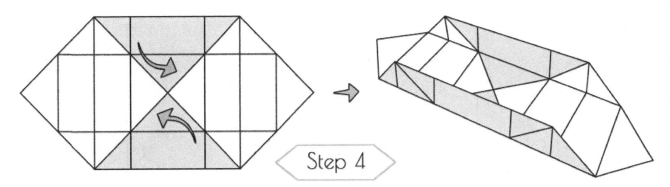

Fold the top and bottom edges up so they end up vertical
to the center of the figure. Repeat on the other sheet.

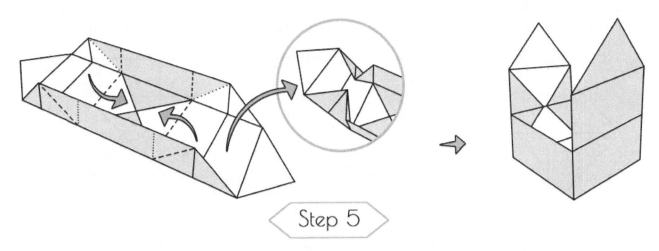

Step 5

Fold both side corners up so they end up vertical as well. As you
do this, you will see a flap form between those sections and the
ones from step 4: fold them inward with a diagonal valley fold
and a vertical mountain fold. Repeat on the other sheet.

Step 6

Fold those sections back
down just above the flaps
that you folded in, then
fold the tips up so that
they end parallel to the
bottom. Repeat on the
other sheet and turn it
over to use it as a lid.

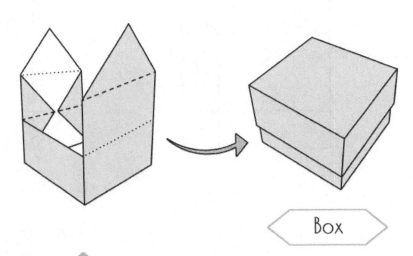

Box

Ninja Star 1

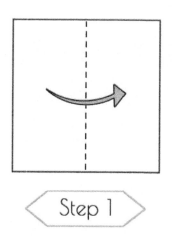

Fold one paper sheet in half lengthwise, then unfold. Repeat with another sheet.

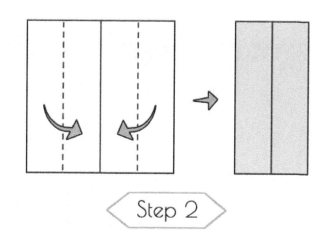

Step 2

Fold each of these halves again in half lengthwise to get two flaps. Repeat with the other sheet.

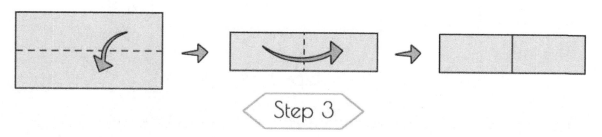

Step 3

Fold both sheets in half lengthwise. Then fold them in half crosswise and unfold.

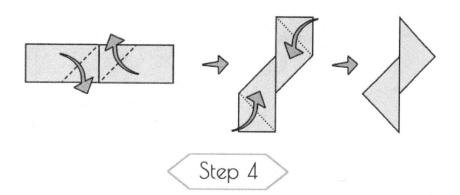

Step 4

Fold the left half of the first sheet down and the right half up. Then fold the top right and bottom left corners back.

Ninja Star 1

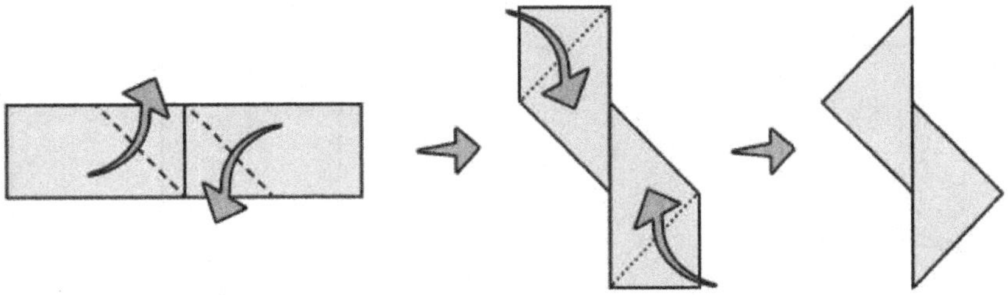

Step 5

Fold the left half of the other sheet up and the right half down. Then fold the top left and bottom right corners back.

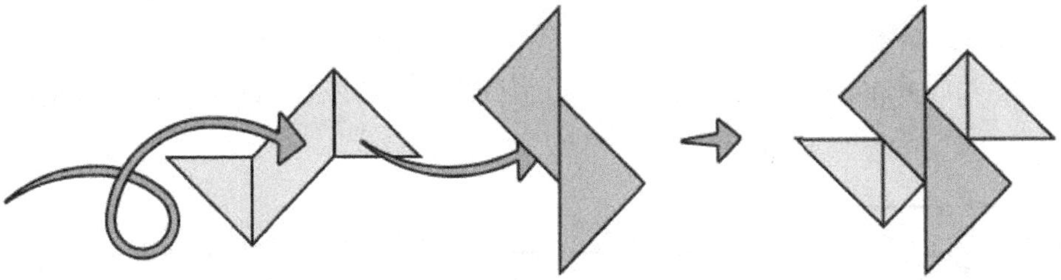

Step 6

Turn one of the figures over and place it on top of the other in an X shape. From now on the two sheets wil be of different shades for clarity.

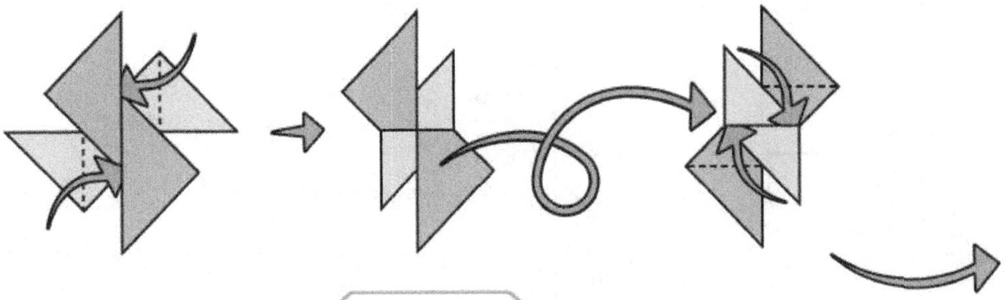

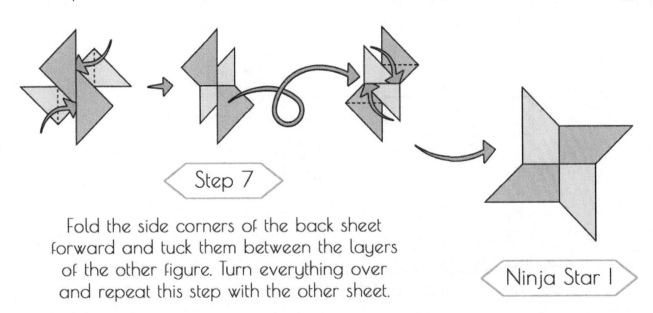

Step 7

Fold the side corners of the back sheet forward and tuck them between the layers of the other figure. Turn everything over and repeat this step with the other sheet.

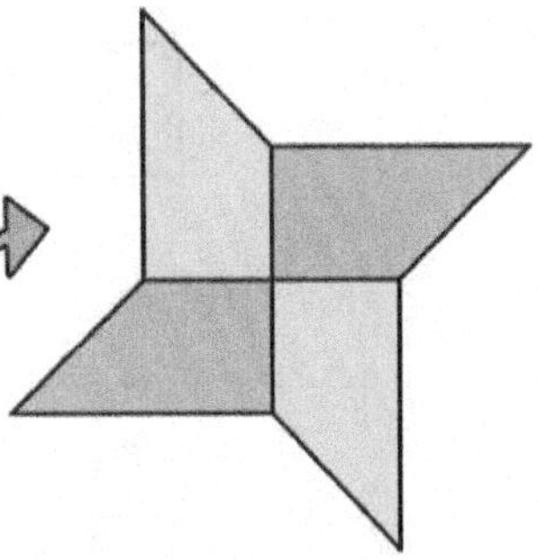

Ninja Star 1

Triceratops

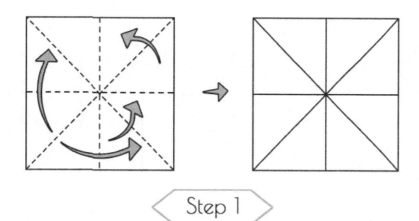

Step 1

Fold in half lengthwise, crosswise, and diagonally, and unfold.

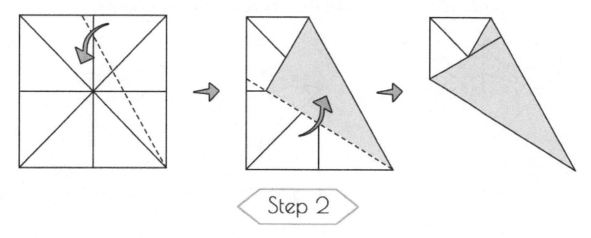

Step 2

Bring the upper right corner to the left side of the horizontal crease.
Then bring the lower left corner to the upper side of the vertical crease

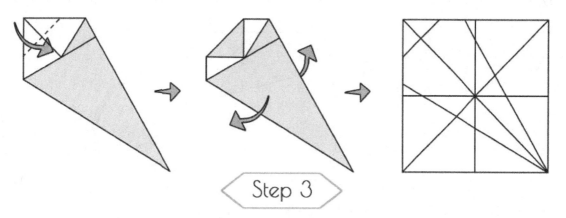

Step 3

Fold the left tip down to the point where the folds from
the previous step meet. Then unfold everything.

Triceratops

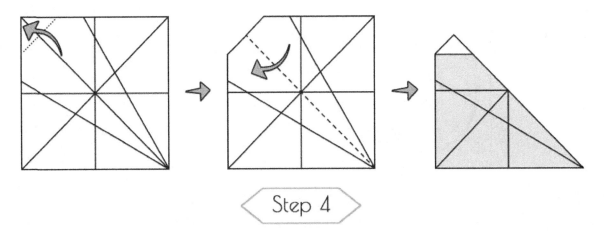

Step 4

Fold the tip again, this time toward the back along the same crease. Then fold the entire figure diagonally.

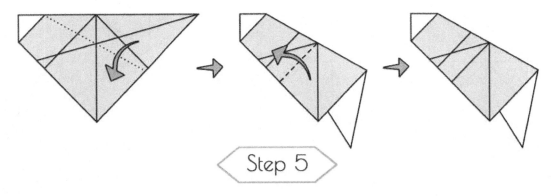

Step 5

Rotate the figure so the top edge is horizontal, and make an inside reverse fold on the right side of the figure as shown. Then fold so that the lower right corner of the top layer meets the lower left corner, and unfold.

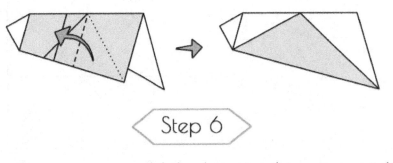

Step 6

Use that crease to fold the lower right corner of the top layer to the left. You will see that part of the inside reverse fold from the previous step unfolds with it, so flatten until you get a triangular flap.

Triceratops

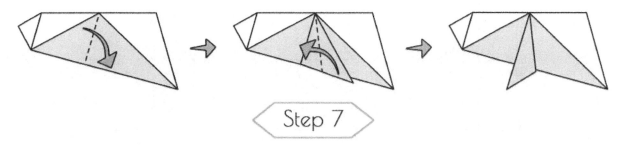

Step 7

Fold the triangular flap back again. Then fold it in half so that its tip sticks out at the bottom edge.

Step 8

Turn the figure over and repeat steps 6 and 7 on the other side.

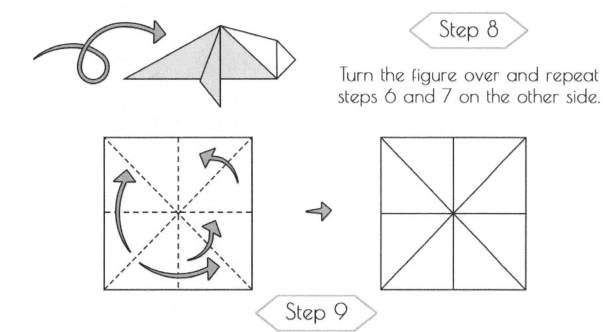

Step 9

Fold another sheet in half lengthwise, crosswise, and diagonally, and unfold.

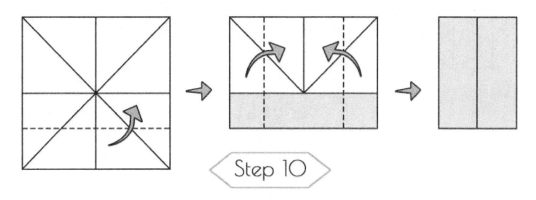

Step 10

Fold the bottom edge up and the side edges inward to the midline.

91

Triceratops

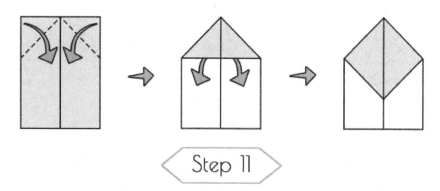

Fold the top corners diagonally inward, then unfold the layer underneath and flatten to get a triangle on each side.

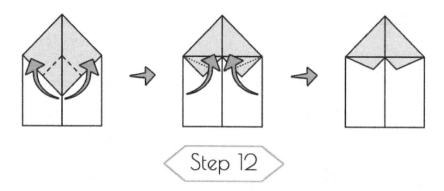

Step 12

Fold diagonally up each side again. Then make an inside reverse fold on each of those side flaps.

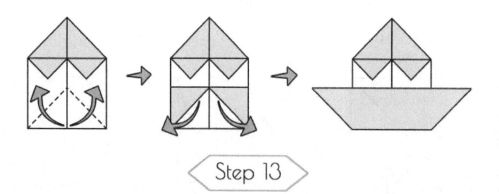

Step 13

Fold the bottom corners diagonally outward. Now carefully separate both sides of the top layer, unfold the layer below and press along the creases you just made (now the layer below should be on top).

Triceratops

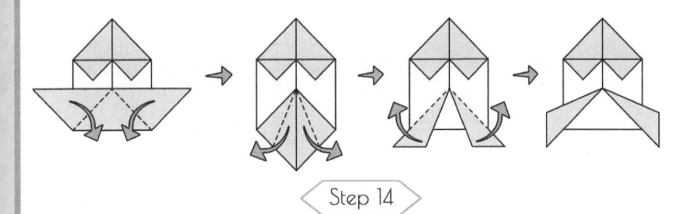

Step 14

Fold the side corners diagonally down. Then
fold them up twice in a row as shown.

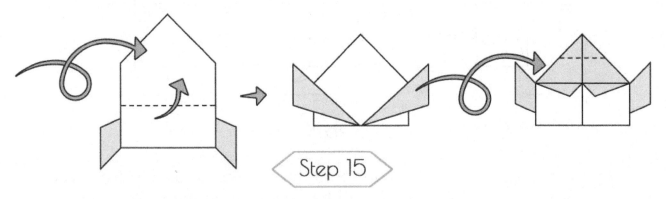

Step 15

Turn the figure over, then fold it up so that the bottom edge
lands right where the triangular shape at the top begins.

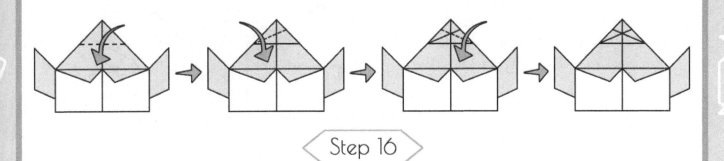

Step 16

Fold the top tip down in half and unfold. Then fold
it to the right, unfold, and to the left, and unfold.

Triceratops

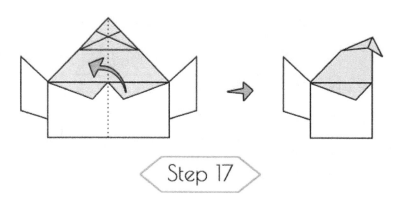

Fold the figure lengthwise in half. At the same time, fold the tip up along the creases from step 16, but only slightly, without pressing it all the way down.

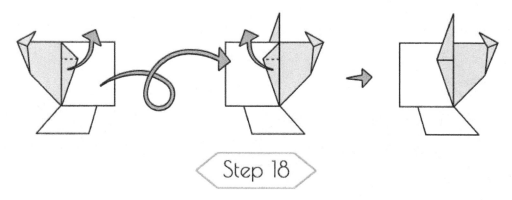

Step 18

Rotate the figure to the side and fold up the triangular flap from step 12. Then turn the figure over and fold the one on the other side up.

Insert the fold on the inside of the head into the flap on the right end of the body to join them!

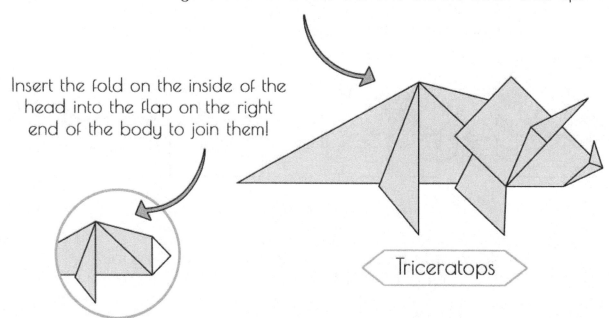

Triceratops

Ninja Star II

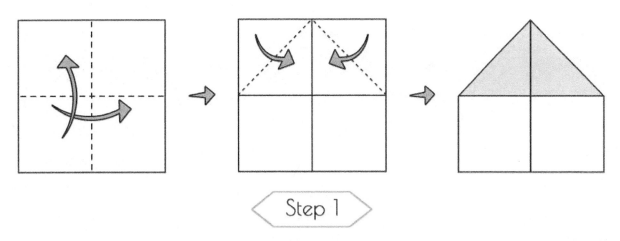

Step 1

Fold in half lengthwise and crosswise, and unfold. Then fold the top corners forward to the center of the sheet. Repeat this step with 7 more sheets.

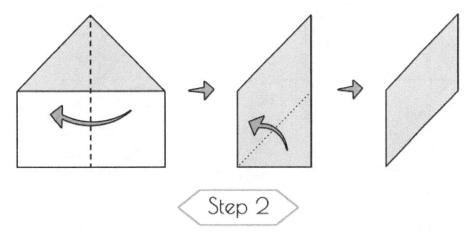

Step 2

Fold in half lengthwise. Then make a diagonal inside reverse fold to tuck the bottom right corner between both layers. Repeat this step with 7 more sheets.

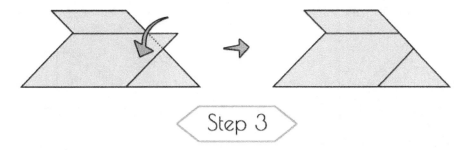

Step 3

Rotate the figure to the left and insert a second figure between the two flaps on the right side so that their bottom edges are aligned. Then fold the tips of the first figure into the flaps of the second so that it stays in place.

Ninja Star II

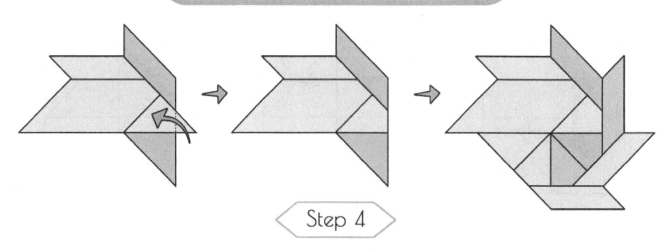

Step 4

Repeat step 3 with a third figure. Keep adding figures until only two are left.

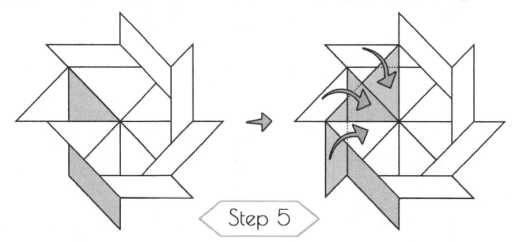

Step 5

Now the tricky part: insert the seventh figure between the flaps of the sixth, but separating its own flaps so that they end over the first figure you placed. Repeat with the eighth figure: insert it between the flaps of the seventh and separate its own so that they end over the first and second figures. Then fold the tips of both figures toward the inside of the corresponding flaps.

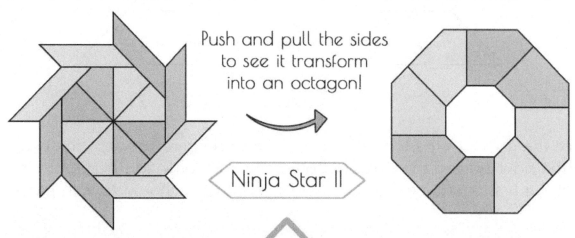

Push and pull the sides to see it transform into an octagon!

Ninja Star II

Magic Circle

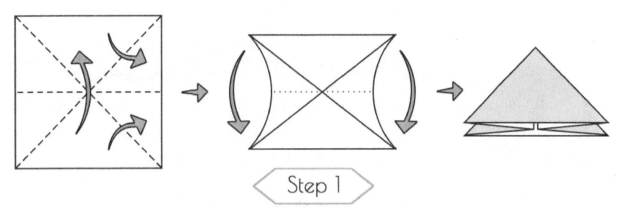

Fold in half crosswise and along the two diagonals, and unfold. Then fold both sides in toward the center and press the edges to make a triangle.

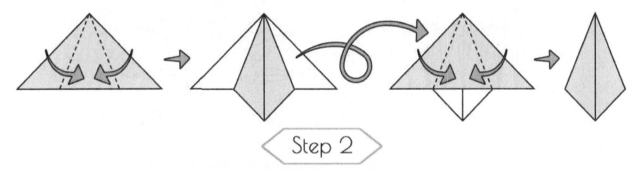

Step 2

Fold the side corners of the top layer toward the midline and press. Turn the figure over and repeat the same step with the back side corners.

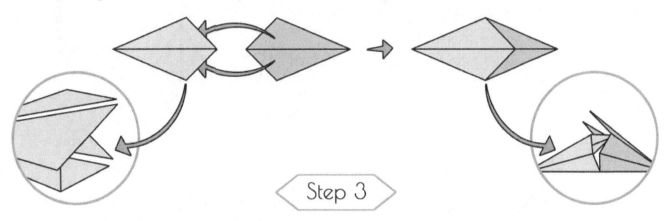

Step 3

Repeat steps 1 and 2 until you have 8 equal figures. Then take two facing each other at the bottom corners. You will see that each corner is made up of two sections with two layers each: insert the tip of each section of the figure on the right between the layers of the tips of the figure on the left. Do this only on one side of the figures, leaving the other side as it was.

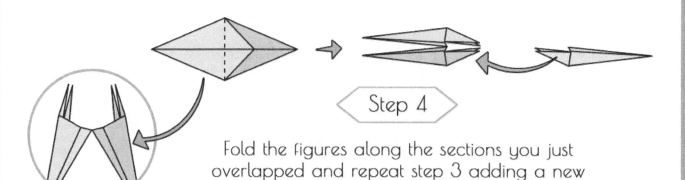

Fold the figures along the sections you just overlapped and repeat step 3 adding a new figure to one of the ends that's still free.

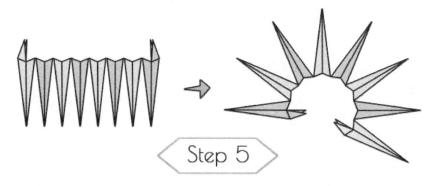

Keep adding pieces until they form a row with the ends free. Then form a circle and join the free ends together.

Ready? Flip the circle from the center out to see the magic happen!

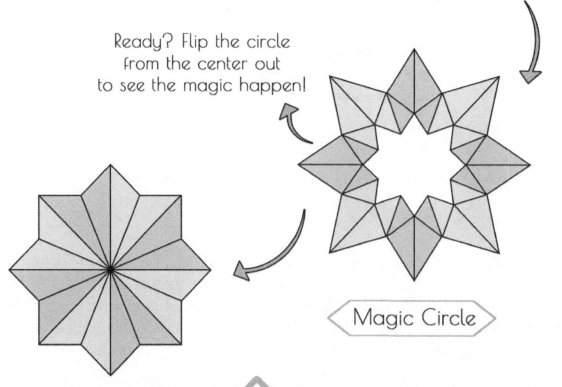

Magic Circle

Water Lily

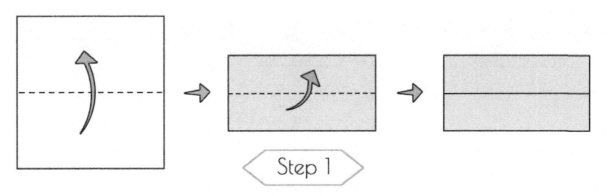

Step 1

Fold in half crosswise. Then fold again crosswise and unfold this part. Repeat this step until you have 16 equal pieces, 8 of them slightly larger than the other 8.

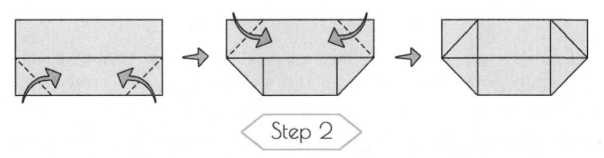

Step 2

Fold the bottom corners diagonally upward. Then fold the top corners, but only from the top layer, diagonally down. Repeat until all 16 figures look the same.

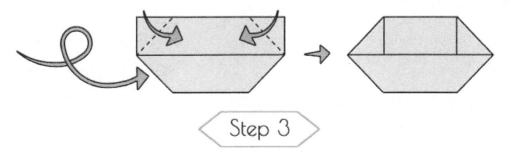

Step 3

Turn the figure over and fold the top corners of the back layer diagonally down. Repeat until all 16 figures look the same.

Water Lily

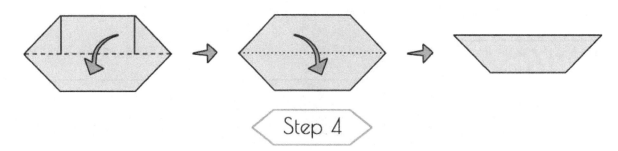

Step 4

Fold the top half of the front layer forward down. Then fold the top half of the back layer backward down. Repeat until all 16 figures look the same.

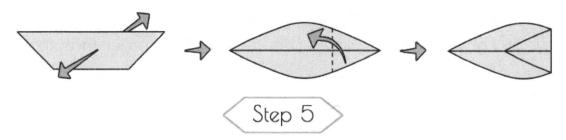

Step 5

Separate both sides of the sheet along the top edge. Then fold one of the side corners inward and press. Repeat for all 16 pieces.

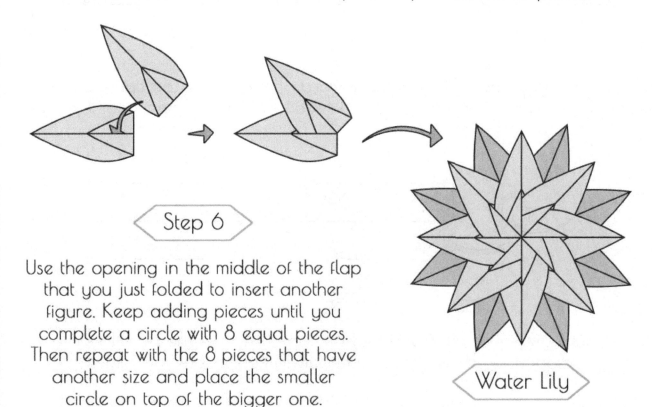

Step 6

Use the opening in the middle of the flap that you just folded to insert another figure. Keep adding pieces until you complete a circle with 8 equal pieces. Then repeat with the 8 pieces that have another size and place the smaller circle on top of the bigger one.

Water Lily

Christmas Tree

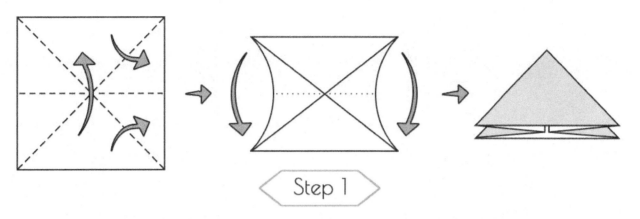

Step 1

Fold in half crosswise and along the two diagonals, and unfold.
Then fold the sides to the center and flatten to get a triangle.
Repeat on three more sheets, each one smaller than the last.

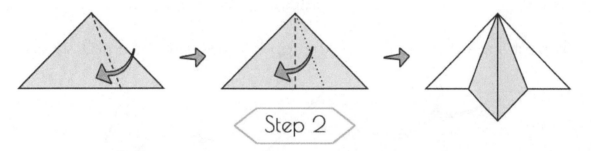

Step 2

Fold the top right side toward the midline and unfold. Then unfold the two
layers of that section following that crease and flatten. Repeat on all sheets.

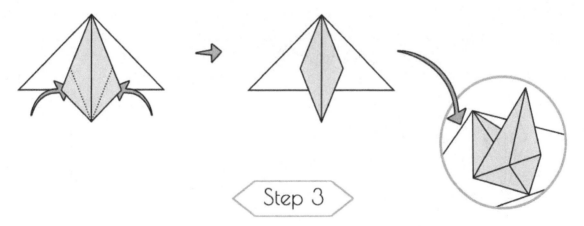

Step 3

Fold the sides in toward the midline, so that the upper edge ends up being
horizontal. Check the 3D view to see how it should look if you fold the
bottom tip up (not part of the process though). Repeat on all sheets.

Christmas Tree

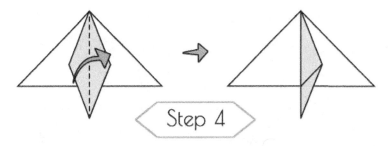

Step 4

Fold that section in half to the right. Repeat on all sheets.

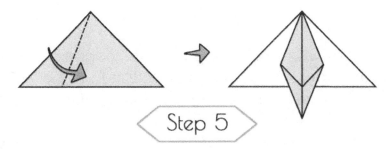

Step 5

Repeat steps 3 through 4 on the top left side. Repeat on all sheets.

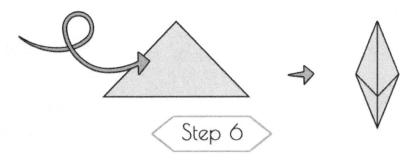

Step 6

Turn the figure over and repeat steps 2 through 4 on the back layer. Repeat on all sheets.

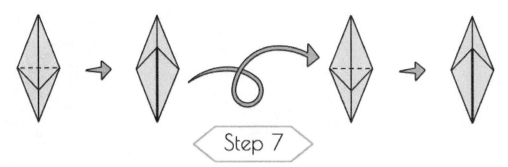

Step 7

Fold up the flap in the center. Then turn the figure over and do the same on the other side. Note that there is an opening between the lower sections on both sides of the figure. Repeat on all sheets.

Christmas Tree

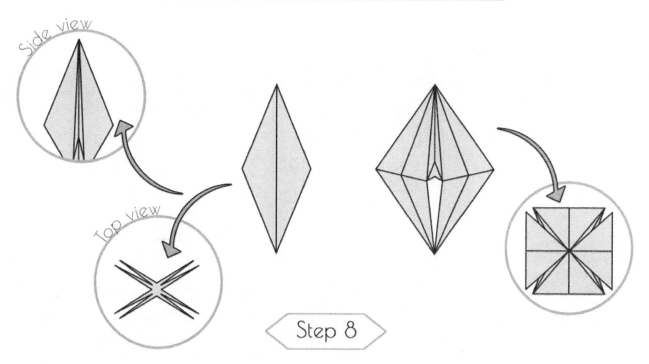

Side view

Top view

Step 8

At this point the figure has four sides with a flap in the center and four blank sides. Hold the figure so that the flap sides are folded and the blank sides are open. Carefully use a skewer or pencil to insert it through the bottom opening of the figure and pop the blank sides out. Repeat on all sheets.

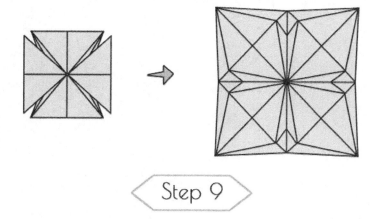

Step 9

Looking at the figure from above, press the center until the figure pops: that top corner will end up pointing in the opposite direction, and the bottom corners will end up pointing up and out. Repeat on all sheets.

Christmas Tree

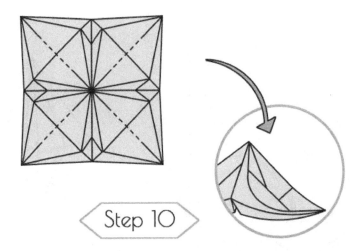

Press the middle of the diagonals, so that they form a ridge that sticks out on the opposite side of the figure. Repeat on all the sheets, then flip them over and lay them one on top of the other from largest to smallest.

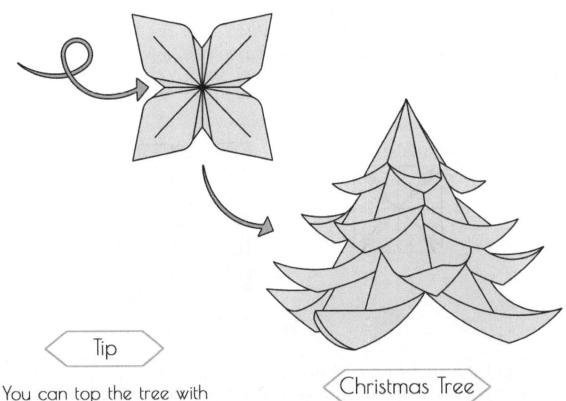

Tip

You can top the tree with the star that you learned to make a few pages ago.

Christmas Tree

Pop-it Triangle

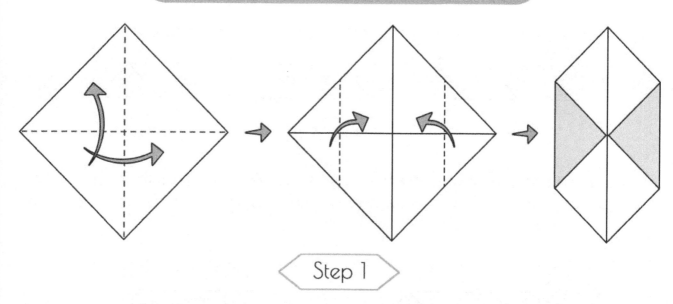

Step 1

Fold along the diagonals, unfold, and bring the side corners to the midline. Repeat on two more sheets.

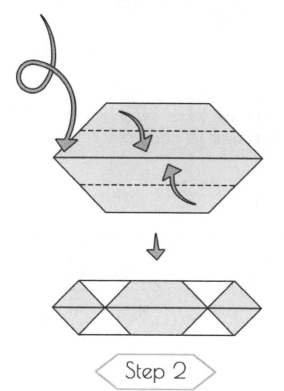

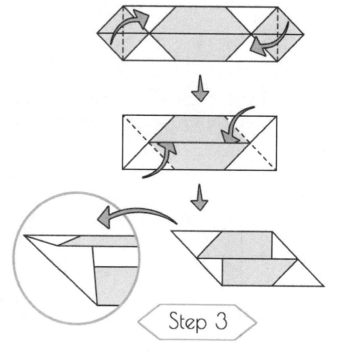

Step 2

Fold the top and bottom edges toward the midline. Repeat on two more sheets.

Step 3

Fold the side corners inward. Then fold the lower left and upper right corners diagonally and tuck them under the top layer on the opposite side. Repeat on two more sheets.

Pop-it Triangle

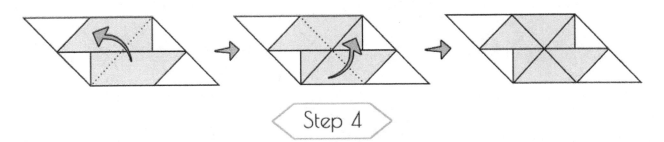

Step 4

Fold the figure diagonally to the left to make a crease and unfold. Then fold to the right to make another crease and unfold. Repeat on the other two sheets.

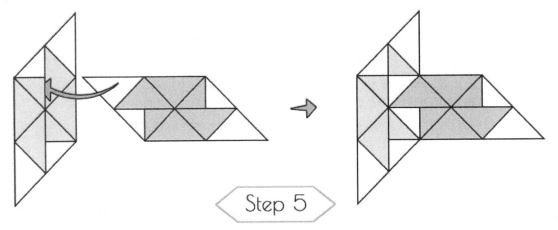

Step 5

Tuck the corner of one figure under the top layer of another as shown, so that they end perpendicular to each other.

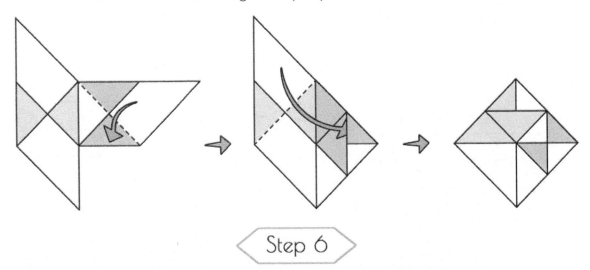

Step 6

Turn everything over and fold the figure on the right diagonally down. Then insert the top corner of the figure on the left just below the tip of the other figure. At the end of this step the entire figure takes a 3D shape.

Pop-it Triangle

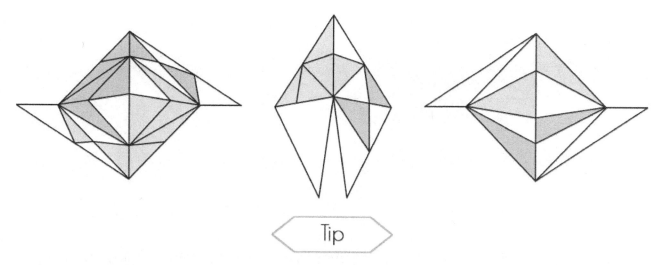

Tip

Before adding the third figure, here's how the layout should look, left to right: from above, from the side, and from below.

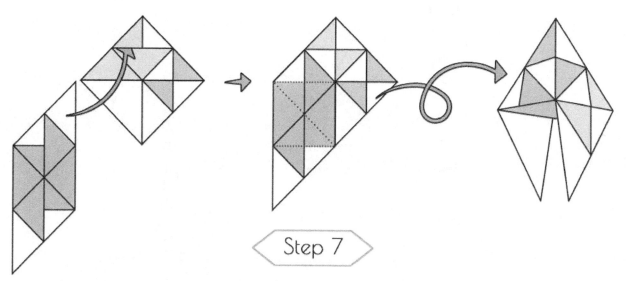

Step 7

Tuck the top tip of the third shape under the top corner of the part that is already assembled. Then fold it so that you can tuck the lower tip under the top corner but on the back side.

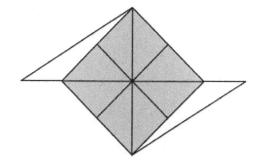

Tip

This is how the figure should look if you turn it over and look at it from below.

Pop-it Triangle

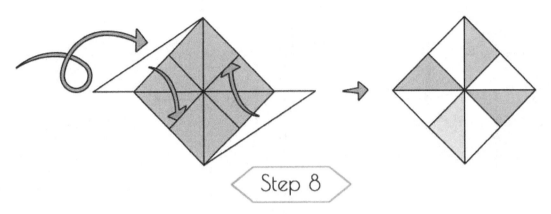

Step 8

Turn the figure over and, looking at its bottom, insert the upper left flap on the left side of the lower corner and the lower right flap on the right side of the upper corner.

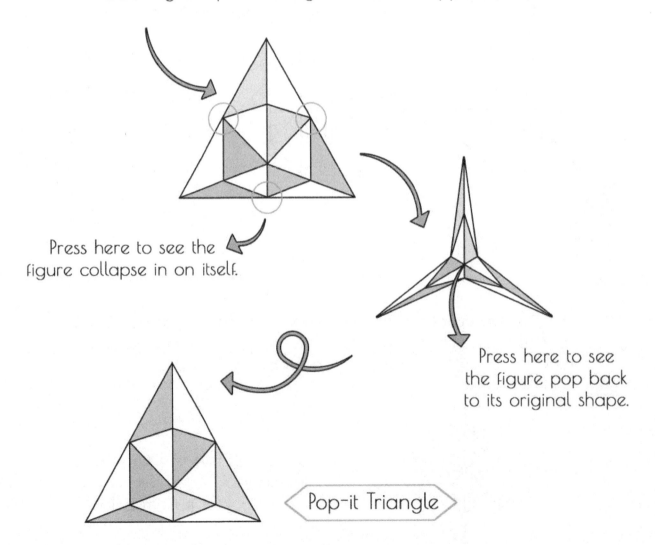

Press here to see the figure collapse in on itself.

Press here to see the figure pop back to its original shape.

Pop-it Triangle

Conclusion

Congratulations on making it to the end of this origami book, I'm sure you are already a master of the art of folding paper! After learning how to fold the animals, vehicles, flowers, and toys that fill these pages, you can jump on the adventure of designing and folding your own creatures to share with your friends and family.

I hope this trip has been fun and you've discovered a hobby as exciting and relaxing at the same time as origami. Are you already thinking about your next project? We sure are! That's why if you have enjoyed this book we would really appreciate your review on Amazon, since it's our way of learning and growing with you, and keep creating fun and quality books like this one.

Made in the USA
Middletown, DE
19 July 2024

57633318R00066